ROADSIDE
REVENANTS

ROADSIDE REVENANTS

AND OTHER NORTH CAROLINA GHOSTS AND LEGENDS

MICHAEL RENEGAR

Bright Mountain Books, Inc.
Fairview, North Carolina

Cover photo © 2005 Michael F. Renegar
Cover model: Stephanie Luffman as Lydia

Printed in the United States of America

ISBN: 0-914875-46-9
EAN: 978-0-914875-46-8

Library of Congress Cataloging-in-Publication Data

Renegar, Michael F., 1969-
   Roadside revenants and other North Carolina ghosts and legends / Michael F. Renegar.
      p. cm.
   ISBN 0-914875-46-9 (pbk.)
   1. Ghosts—North Carolina. 2. Haunted places—North Carolina. I. Title.

BF1472.U6R46 2005
133.109756--dc22

2005027076

To Dad and Mom, Flay and Katie Renegar
Thanks for always believing

Contents

ROADSIDE REVENANTS

Introduction

Ghost. The word conjures up images of fleeting apparitions, the sounds of footsteps from unseen feet, and the tingly feel of a chill along one's spine. It is a subject that has fascinated and frightened people from the very beginning of our species.

There are many names for those who haunt the living. Apparition, haint, phantom, shade, spook, wraith–all are used to mean ghost. Another word sometimes used is revenant, meaning "one who comes back from the grave." A revenant has the distinct personality of a specific person, now dead, and interacts with its surroundings, including living people. There is usually a specific reason for the presence of a revenant, and when that purpose is accomplished, the revenant will disappear–most of the time, though not always.

Vanishing hitchhikers are a type of revenant, with the specified purpose of getting home to loved ones. It is assumed that, should anyone ever actually manage to reunite one of these poor shades with its family, the ghost would cease its roaming. To my knowledge, though, not one of the myriad hitchers has made it all the way home. So many of the ghost stories in this collection take place alongside roads, paths, and highways, that Roadside Revenants seemed a fitting title.

I've studied ghost stories since I was a child. I can remember sitting, mesmerized, as relatives, grandparents, and friends told ghost stories. Some were even harrowing personal adventures. As I grew up, I began to doubt these old tales. As a teenager I barely thought about them. In 1987, I went to Appalachian State University in Boone, North Carolina, and rediscovered ghosts. Things haven't been the same since.

While at Appalachian, I organized a group of friends who became known as the Ghost Chasers. So many strange incidents occurred that we just had to try to find out the truth for ourselves. In groups of from two to twelve, we visited "haunted" places. I ended up doing so much research I wrote an article called "Shadows in the Mist" for Appalachian's Equinox magazine in the spring of 1992. Some of the stories in this book are the experiences of the Ghost Chasers. At one point I lived in a haunted residence hall and kept a journal of the ghostly incidents. A few of the tales here are from my journal.

Some of these stories are generations old, while others are a more recent vintage. Though I've changed some of the names to protect privacy, each of these stories has two things in common: real places and real events. The ancient hills and mountains of northwestern North Carolina contain a wealth of history and folklore. Daniel Boone explored the region. The Jack tales originated here. Tom Dula (Dooley) walked these hills and supposedly committed the crime that became the basis for a song.

In some of the more remote regions, children still can't come out of their houses at night for fear of the "bogeyman." Few of the superstitious and private people will discuss haints,

as they call them, with strangers. I fear some of these magnifi-
cent stories will vanish, which is why I've set out to collect and
put onto paper as many of the surviving tales as I can. I don't
want to see our traditions fade.

Most of the sites written about here are private or restricted
property. Don't go snooping around without proper permission
or you could wind up in jail.

I hope you enjoy these stories. And don't worry about that
unnatural whisper from just behind you, or that soft, cold touch
on your shoulder. It's probably nothing.

The Priest Didn't Do It

St. John the Baptist Episcopal Church, Valle Crucis
Watauga County

Valle Crucis is a quiet village, named after the cross formed by the rivers there, in the North Carolina mountains. Located on old N.C. 194, the town is best known for the Mast General Store, Camp Broadstone, and St. John the Baptist Episcopal Church. The small, wooden church sits on an isolated knoll, accessible only by a dirt road.

The Episcopal Church opened St. John's more than a century ago, but its congregation has moved on. The nearby Church of the Holy Cross cares for the building, using it during the summer and for special services.

And a ghost lives there.

The legend of the old church is that many years ago, a fresh, young priest arrived at St. John's with visions of reviving the congregation. The priest's new ways and ideas didn't go over with the simple folk of Valle Crucis. Attendance at the church fell until only a handful of people showed up for services. The priest couldn't understand why he'd failed. Depression overwhelmed

5

him, and one day he took a rope, fashioned a noose, and hanged himself either from the bell tower or on a limb of one of the three big trees in front of the church. Now his broken-hearted spirit wanders around St. John's, still trying to understand why his congregation left.

The story has been retold for so long that it's become a popular legend.

Unfortunately the story is simply not true. It has likely been created based on assumptions concerning St. John's founding clergyman, the Reverend William West Skiles, who was neither new nor young when he came to Valle Crucis and St. John's. Skiles didn't drive away his congregation with his fresh views. He didn't commit suicide. He didn't even die in Valle Crucis. Father Skiles died in Linville while caring for an ill church member. His body was returned to Valle Crucis and is buried on the grounds at St. John's.

Does that mean there is no ghost at the old church? It may not be a spectral, suicidal clergyman, but something strange goes on there. Too many people have seen and heard things that can't easily be explained. And whatever it is, it scares the daylights out of people! Strange tapping noises, bumps, and hollow footsteps have been heard. Eerie lights have been seen. One group of Appalachian State University students left the church in a hurry when every one of their flashlights went out at the same time.

Another student drove his girlfriend out to Valle Crucis after dinner one night. Dusk had fallen, but there was still enough light to see. Mitch turned down the old dirt road that led to St. John's and parked near some bushes close to the church. He smiled at Rhonda as he shut the car off, then he leaned over to kiss her.

Rhonda gasped. "Look!"

"What? What?" Mitch jerked away from her; afraid at first she was angry.

"There's a man watching us!"

"Where?"

Rhonda pointed out the window. "At the church!"

Mitch saw a man standing on the steps of the old church. Though he couldn't make out details of the man's face, Mitch could tell he had been disgusted by what the two young people had been about to do. The man wore a black hat and black coat. He turned and walked into the church.

Guilt stabbed through Mitch. He hadn't meant to offend anyone. He hadn't even realized they'd parked so close to the church. He said to Rhonda, "Must be a priest from Holy Cross. I'd better go apologize."

Rhonda protested. She was nervous and wanted to leave, but Mitch got out and walked over to the church. The lights were on inside, so he walked up the stairs and went in. The old church was empty.

"Hello," he called. "Hello, Reverend?"

There was no answer.

Mitch looked around, walked to the pulpit, turned and faced the pews, but there was no one there. The door was unlocked, the lights were on, he'd seen the man go inside, so how could the place be empty?

As he stood there, Mitch felt coldness creep around him. It encircled him, entered him, and made the hair on the back of his neck stand up. "I'm sorry for what you saw!" he blurted. Icy fear came over Mitch. He turned and ran out of the church.

"What happened?" Rhonda asked as he jumped into the car.

Mitch turned the key as fast as he could. "I apologized," he muttered as he slammed the car into reverse. He didn't tell her he'd apologized to an empty church.

Just before he drove off, Mitch looked back. The lights from inside were off. The man in black stood on the steps, watching. Mitch stomped on the gas.

Whatever Mitch and Rhonda saw that night, and whatever others have seen and heard, has become part of the legend of St. John's. That legend will remain, probably to the caretaker's chagrin, for as long as the church stands.

Phantom Headlights

Near Yadkinville
Yadkin County

Folklore is filled with stories of phantom horsemen, vanishing hitchhikers, ghostly animals, and so forth. There are also many reports of inanimate objects from the past reappearing years after they were destroyed. The phantom train at Bostian's bridge, and the famous Old 97 near Va. 58 in Virginia are good examples, as is the spectral wagon that careens down an old trail at Stone Mountain, North Carolina, near Traphill.

Why do these objects show up? They cannot be ghosts themselves, at least, not in the traditional sense. After all, these machines never possessed a living soul to "return from the grave." Perhaps there is some credence lent to the "temporal recording" theory concerning some paranormal phenomena, which offers that "ghosts" are simply some sort of recording of a traumatic or momentous event upon a particular spot. Then again, maybe these sounds and visions are detected simply because they are a part of the memory of the revenant causing the haunting. The object played a part in the final moments of life, so the ghost projects it from its psyche.

Whatever the cause, one such spectral vehicle sweeps along a road near Yadkinville. It is a ghostly car, manifested by phantom headlights. People say that if you drive down to the dead end (no pun intended) and turn around, the spook car will pursue you back to the end of the road. Neither the car itself nor its revenant driver are ever seen, but the ethereal set of headlights will follow closely, stopping when you stop, speeding up when you do, chasing you at whatever pace you set, and disappearing at the juncture with Hoots Road. Though the car and driver are never seen, the motor can be heard racing, and a hollow-sounding horn has been heard to blare.

Legend tells that one night, a reckless man led police on a high-speed chase. He sped down the road, not realizing it came to an abrupt end. The law was hot on his tail, so he sped up as he crossed a small bridge and raced up the hill. Suddenly, the dead end loomed before him!

The fugitive tried to stop, but it was too late. His car crashed through the barricade and into the trees. He was killed instantly, his neck broken. The officers who'd been chasing him could see, in the moonlight, a huge cross formed by the trees over the scene. Unnerved, they waited in their vehicles for emergency workers to arrive.

Precisely why our reckless fugitive was running from the law is pure conjecture. Some say he was running moonshine. Others said he was speeding and just wanted to get away. Still others believed he was a wanted man and had nothing to lose. Whatever his motives, the man paid with his life. And apparently he remains there, chasing away anyone who happens upon the place of his untimely demise.

Jenny and Cathy had heard the stories. One night, on a dare, the two girls decided to go looking for the ghost. It was a moonlit night, with no clouds. Slowly, the girls approached the dead end road–one of several area roads named for an assassinated United States president–in Jenny's Ford Mustang.

Jenny pulled over to the shoulder of Hoots Road and looked at her friend. "Are you sure about this?" she asked.

"Are you kidding?" Cathy demanded. "We'll never hear the end of it if we wimp out now! And we'd have to give Emily ten dollars each! What's more, she'd gloat forever! Do you really want to hear her mouth for the next few months until we blow this berg for college? I don't! Let's just get it done!"

"All right, if you say so," Jenny said, pulling back onto the road and turning onto the dead end lane. "Here we go!"

The Mustang advanced down the narrow dirt road. They went down the hill, crossed the one-lane bridge, and climbed the opposite hill. Finally, it began to level off, and they picked up some speed. Suddenly, an old barricade with faded paint loomed ahead. Both girls screamed as Jenny slammed on the brakes. The car skidded and came to a stop—inches from the barricade!

The girls regained their composure, and sighs of relief escaped both. "Whew!" Cathy gasped. "That was close!"

"Sure was!" Jenny agreed. "If the story is true, I can see why the poor guy wrecked!"

"Oh my God, Jenny, look!" a wide-eyed Cathy cried, pointing out the windshield. The other girl peered up. Illuminated in the headlights and moonlight was a perfectly formed cross, created by the trees. Both girls felt a chill race up their spines.

"Uh, . . . well . . ." Jenny coughed. "We know that much is true. Ready to find out if the rest is?"

"This place gives me the creeps!" Cathy replied. "I don't care if it is or not! Let's just get out of here!"

Jenny put the car in reverse and turned around. She shifted into drive and muttered under her breath, "here goes nothin'!"

The car began to move. Both girls tensed. Would some spook car pop up behind them and give chase? They started back down the hill. Nothing seemed out of the ordinary. The two young women relaxed.

Just then, bright headlights appeared in the mirrors and glowed through the back window. The lights came up on the Mustang's bumper rapidly. Through the dust and glare, they could not make out what kind of car it was, but the lights were set wide apart, like an older model. "What the heck?" Jenny demanded.

"It's him! It's him! Oh my God, it's really him!" Cathy bellowed as she half-turned to look through the back window. "I can't see any car, Jen! It's just lights!"

Jenny stomped the gas pedal, and the car shot forward, fishtailing wildly. Even more dust flew up, obscuring the pursuing lights, and they receded temporarily. Seconds later, however, they were right back on her bumper. The unseen car seemed intent on ramming them. Jenny hit the bottom of the hill, raced across the bridge and up the opposite side. The ghost car remained glued to their tail. Cathy rolled down her window and stuck her head out to look behind them. She could hear both motors, but all she could see of their pursuer were those eerie headlights.

The phantom driver apparently saw her, however. He flashed his lights to low, to high, to low, and back to high. A horn blared in the night air, but it sounded funny—distant and muffled, as if filtered through something. Perhaps through the mists of time itself.

Jenny slowed as they neared the intersection with Hoots Road. Their pursuer slowed too, matching their speed exactly. The Mustang did not stop completely, but skidded out onto Hoots and headed towards U.S. 601, accelerating to get away. Jenny looked up in her rearview mirror just in time to see the headlights wink out of existence. There was no sign that anything had ever been behind them. The ghost car had vanished at the intersection, just like the legend said!

They didn't go back for a closer look. Both girls had had enough and firmly believed in the presence of the phantom headlights. They glanced at each other as the car pulled onto U.S. 601 headed for town. They drove in silence.

The girls pulled into the parking lot of McDonald's to find Emily and some of their other friends waiting for them. "Well?" Emily demanded as they got out. "Did you see it?"

"Yes," Jenny replied. "We saw it. It's all true!"

"I don't believe it!" Emily declared. "You guys are too chicken to have gone down there! Let's go back down there right now!"

"Not on your life, Ems!" Cathy growled sharply. "I believe in ghosts now, and I don't need another dose to be convinced!"

"Chickens!" Emily teased.

"If you're so brave, why don't you go there by yourself?" Jenny shot back.

The color drained from the other girl's face. "Uh, no, that's okay." Emily said softly. "I guess you did see it . . . just like I did. Here's your money."

"Keep it," Jenny told her. "I just want to forget this night ever happened!"

She didn't forget, of course. Who could forget being chased by a ghost? Jenny doesn't talk about it, though. Cathy, however, is more than happy to discuss it. She is the one who gave me this story, in fact. She has come to be very much interested in investigating paranormal activity. In the past ten years, Cathy has visited several of the most famous haunted sites in the country, including the Winchester House in California, the St. James Hotel in New Mexico, ghost lights in Marfa, Texas, as well as North Carolina's infamous Devil's Tramping Ground, Maco Station, Brown Mountain, and the haunted underpass near Jamestown where the tragic Lydia is said to appear. Her favorite story, however, remains the one that introduced her to ghost chasing—the one who once chased her.

The Hound

Valle Crucis
Watauga County

No, this isn't the English moors and Sherlock Holmes isn't on the case. This story comes from the area near St. John the Baptist Episcopal Church in Valle Crucis.

Melanie was an honest, level-headed person. She didn't believe in ghosts. She'd heard the stories about the strange goings-on at St. John's, and she was determined to prove there was nothing unusual happening there. One night in the spring of 1992, Melanie borrowed her boyfriend's car and drove to Valle Crucis. Unwisely, she went alone.

As she drove through the mist on the winding N.C. 194, Melanie began to wonder what she would do if the stories were somehow true. When she reached the dirt road that led to the church, her courage fled. She decided to turn around.

The mist was really rolling now. She stopped her car, turned around, and drove back over the bridge she'd just passed. A chill touched her heart. She was being watched. She knew it as well as she knew her own name. Though she didn't want to, she slowly

15

turned her head and looked out her window.

And almost wrecked.

For there, running beside her, pacing the car at forty-five miles per hour, was a huge, black dog! Its massive head stood at her eye level; its breath fogged the outside of the window. Its teeth bared in a vicious snarl.

Melanie screamed. She tried to press the gas pedal through the floorboard.

The dog leaped. It passed through the front of the car, then vanished. Melanie looked all around her, but there was nothing there.

She drove home in a daze. Later she recalled the dog looked like a cross between a Rottweiler and a bear.

There is some background to what Melanie saw. Some people know of a "Broadstone Hound," while others speak of the "Hell Hound." No one who's ever seen it can forget it.

A young man named Thad was riding with some friends who'd been visiting at Lees-McRae College in Banner Elk. They were driving to Boone and decided to take N.C. 194 through Valle Crucis instead of 105. They even decided to stop at St. John's.

Their car wound down the mountain through a light fog. The boys talked about their friends, about girls, and about ghosts. They approached the last big curve just above the Holy Cross Mission when the headlights illuminated something in the road.

A huge, black dog stood in the curve. It looked similar to a Rottweiler and stood as tall as the car. It stared at them, except for one thing—here were no eyeballs. The dog's eye sockets were empty.

All the boys gasped. The driver braked hard, but other than going off the side of the mountain, there was no way to avoid hitting it. Thad got a good look at the dog in that last second before impact. He described it as: "Eyeless sockets, huge, black nose, brown cheeks, and massive, sharp, canine teeth! At least five feet tall!"

The boys braced for a jarring impact, but there was none. The car skidded through the dog. It stopped just feet from the precipice and oblivion. The boys looked back. The dog had vanished.

According to Thad, "We forgot about St. John's. We went straight home."

Is it a real dog these people saw, or is it a Hell Hound? If you're driving up that way at night, you'd better stay in the car.

"Do That!"

Elkin
Surry County

Police officers are highly trained professionals, putting their lives on the line day and night to keep the rest of us safe and the criminal element at bay. Often, they are overworked and underpaid, and rarely do they get the thanks or recognition they truly deserve. Most, at some point, have confronted, up close, the human face of evil. Their training shows them how to deal with this. Nothing in their training, however, prepares them for how to deal with otherworldly activity.

One police officer in Elkin, North Carolina, knows this all too well. Several years ago, after only about a year on the force, Rob had a frightening encounter with the unknown in, of all places, a church. At his request, I will not use Rob's last name, nor will I identify the church in question. It still has a fairly large and active congregation, and I do not wish this story to have an adverse effect on these people.

As our hero remembers, it was a very quiet night. There were few calls and very little radio chatter. Nothing seemed amiss in the sleeping little hamlet. A dispatcher, Dawn, and some officers, including Rob and his veteran colleagues Chris and Mike, were on duty. The three men were out on routine patrol, checking on businesses and making sure the town was safe and secure.

At around 2 a.m., Mike made a call over his radio. He'd found a door standing open at one of the town's oldest churches. Suspecting a possible prowler, he requested backup. Rob, closer than anyone else, went to his assistance.

The church is a massive structure of whitewashed bricks. It stands on a narrow avenue under several tall trees. From the backside, this sprawling edifice looks more like some ancient tsarist palace or castle than a place of worship. There were few lights as Rob drove down the narrow lane.

The officer found his colleague waiting outside the building. At the top of a set of metal steps, Rob could see a door standing wide open. The two policemen turned on their flashlights, climbed the stairs, and cautiously entered the church.

According to policy, they did not turn on the lights in the building. They moved about slowly, shining their lights around the sanctuary, and began to search the premises. Hall by hall, alcove by alcove, room by room, they thoroughly searched the entire church, communicating in whispered tones, or with gestures with their flashlights.

Rob recalls that their search took quite a while. He felt it took nearly an hour. They found many valuable items unsecured, such as computers, and sound and musical equipment. Finding no one else in the building, and with nothing seemingly out of place, they decided to call it clear and report in, sending word to a keyholder that they should come and lock up.

They did not use their radios, according to department policy. Many people in the area owned police/emergency scanners, and should somebody with illegal designs be listening, using the radio might alert them to the situation. Should the keyholder fail to come lock up, the church might be cleaned out. Accordingly, the officers went looking for a phone to call the station. They split up.

Rob went down a hallway. He saw a dim light on the wall at the end and figured there was a phone there. Other than this dim glow and his own flashlight, it was pitch black. There was indeed a phone. Rob picked it up and dialed the dispatcher.

As he talked to her, explaining the situation, the policeman began to sense that he was not alone. Suddenly, every hair on him, from head to toe, stood on end. He knew he was being watched. His throat went dry. He had the sensation that someone was just inches behind him, leaning forward over his shoulder. The feeling was so strong, he believed that if he turned his eyes in that direction he would see a face!

The air seemed electrified, and he felt a tingle creeping down his spine. He felt numb and frozen in place. He could not move. It was as if someone or some . . . thing . . . had the drop on him, and he was powerless to do anything about it.

"I'll call the minister and have him meet you there to lock up," the dispatcher told him.

What happened next chilled Rob's very blood and continues to send shivers up his spine to this day. For, on the phone, a deep, extremely unpleasant, sinister—even evil—voice rasped, "Do that!"

His paralysis broken, Rob dropped the phone and took off. He ran down the hall, shouting out to his fellow officer. He got out of the church as quickly as he could. Thinking his colleague had found someone, Mike came running.

Mike found his comrade outside, obviously shaken. He was breathless, trembling, and white as a sheet. When Rob explained what had happened, Mike was skeptical, but it was obvious that something had spooked the other officer. They waited outside for the minister.

It wasn't long before the minister arrived with the key. Without going into detail, Rob told him he'd had a funny feeling inside. The clergyman shrugged it off, locked the door after checking to be sure nothing was missing, and they left.

Rob returned to the station, which was then off Main Street. He was unsettled. The others didn't quite seem to believe it, which only exacerbated matters. The officer knew that all calls in to the department were recorded and kept for future reference. He got the tape and played back the recording, copying it. "Do that!" the sinister voice growled at the appropriate spot, making him jump. It was on the tape! Rob went white. He quickly gathered his associates. They continued to chide him and laugh good-naturedly. Their laughter ceased and the grins died on their faces, however, when Rob played back the tape. For they too heard the dark voice speak, "Do that!" Rob said they all went pale then. Pale as, well, ghosts!

About seven years had passed between the time of this incident and my interview with Rob, now a ranking officer in the Elkin Police Department. "It was the most awful, helpless feeling," he told me. "I don't know quite how to describe it. I know it's something I never want to feel again."

I know that feeling well. I felt it myself, many years ago, when I was at Appalachian State University. Only those who have experienced something of this nature (or un-nature) can truly sympathize with how it can affect you. "You'd be hard pressed to get me back in there at night," Rob told me. "It's not a matter, really, of being scared, I just don't want to feel that weird sensation again."

Rob isn't the only one to have weird experiences in the church. On another occasion, a different officer was in the church. He passed through a genuine cold spot. And the very night of his own encounter, Rob happened to go over to Hugh Chatham Memorial Hospital, where he knew a nurse on duty.

Rob asked her if she'd ever heard anything weird about the old church. The now-retired nurse had, in fact, heard stories. She told him lots of strange things had been told of the place. She had been there herself and felt quite uneasy. She informed him that she had the feeling that something terrible had happened there in the past, perhaps before the church was built.

I drove around the place after our interview, though. It was daytime, but there was a good fog. The tall trees of the surrounding woods made it seem darker, too. And I had a sense of foreboding as I circled around it. That door, though shut, made me uneasy too. Maybe I was keyed up because I had just heard Rob's story, a familiar feeling for people who have been discussing ghost stories. Or, perhaps something was watching . . .

Max

Coffey Residence Hall, Appalachian State University, Boone
Watauga County

Coffey Hall is one of the oldest surviving buildings on the Appalachian State University campus. It is the Honors Residence Hall and once housed single faculty. In such an old building, it isn't surprising to find stories of a ghost.

The main events have happened on the third floor, with Room 311 as the center. The ghost is called Max. Supposedly Max is the shade of a faculty member who committed suicide in the building, although there's no confirmation such an event ever actually occurred. Most of Max's activities are small pranks: doors opening and closing, objects changing places. He has even been said to have stolen girls' underwear at times, which makes him sound more like the ghost of a male student rather than a faculty member.

Martha and Natalie lived in Coffey Hall for two years near Room 311. In the fall of 1987, the two freshmen moved into their suite, which included a bedroom, bathroom, and kitchen-ette. According to Martha, about two weeks after their arrival,

"One night we were sitting there watching TV. All of a sudden, the door just swung open. I'd locked it about twenty minutes before."

Natalie added, "We stared at the empty doorway for a moment. Then the darn thing swung shut again. I was wigged out!"

This was one of Max's favorite tricks. Martha said, "Max never really scared me, but he sure could embarrass me. One time I was changing clothes, and he opened the door just as I was taking my clothes off." Martha confessed another time she and her boyfriend were alone in the room. "We were half-naked, and all of a sudden the door came open! 'Max, shut the door!' I cried. And he did."

Once Natalie was cooking when the water came on. She turned it off, but as soon as she turned away it came back on. She grew annoyed and said, "Quit it, Max. I don't have time for that now." The water stayed off.

Both girls experienced times when they were in the bathroom and the toilet would suddenly flush and the light go out.

One night Martha lay in her bed, just at the point of drifting off to sleep. Someone blew gently in her ear. She opened her eyes and lashed out with her fist. No one was there.

Another night Natalie lay in her bed, sleeping. A gentle tug at her nightgown awakened her. She looked over at Martha, who was sound asleep across the room. Natalie closed her eyes and something pulled her gown again, this time harder. She bolted up. "Max," she said, "please don't touch me again. That scares me." She lay back down. The ghost never touched her again.

Max later redeemed himself. Natalie had a boy over from her history class. The boy kept trying to get close to Natalie, ignoring her protests. She felt she was in real trouble. "Suddenly the bathroom door flew open, the toilet flushed, and the lights in there came on. That guy got white as a sheet! He gathered his stuff and left very quickly, without a word. I said, 'Way to go, Max!'"

The noises, doors opening and closing, and light tricks continued throughout their two years on the third floor. When they moved to the second floor, Max didn't follow.

Near the end of her final year at Appalachian State, Martha went up to the third floor to take a last look around. She stood in the empty hall and said, "Good-bye, Max. I'm graduating, so I'm through here."

The door to her old room swung open, then shut. Martha knew Max had bid her farewell.

There have been other ghostly reports from Coffey Hall. The shady form of a woman has been seen floating outside the upper floor windows, but she hasn't made a confirmed appearance in recent years.

A tale once existed that Coffey was built on a cemetery. LeVerne Foxx, a former driver for Appalachian's founder, B. B. Dougherty, and a lifetime resident of Boone, shattered this myth. Foxx helped build Coffey. He said the cemetery never extended that far down the hill. Part of an old cemetery for African-Americans may have been disturbed to make way for Cone Hall, White Hall, and the road that runs up the hill between them. To date, there have been no documented incidents of ghosts in either of those dormitories.

If you enter the third floor of Coffey Hall, look for Max. He still walks the halls, occasionally teasing with his spectral, lingerie-stealing hands.

John Jackson Mays:
The Hanged Man

Devotion Community
Surry County

It was November 11, 1898. Though no one knew it then, this would be the last public execution in Surry County.

The crowd milled about restlessly. A low murmur of anticipation ran through them. The noise increased when the condemned man appeared, led by the sheriff and a deputy.

People gawked and spoke softly to each other, some satisfied that justice had been served, others sure this execution was wrong. The prisoner had said all along he was innocent. The crowd wondered what he would say today.

The lawmen led the prisoner, John Jackson "Jack" Mays, past his coffin and up the steps to the scaffold. There Jack turned and faced the crowd. A preacher gave a brief sermon, then the crowd sang an old hymn, "Did Christ o'er sinners weep?" Jack joined in the singing.

Then it was time. The sheriff positioned Jack over the trap door, bound his hands and feet, and asked, "Do you have anything to say?"

Jack nodded. He cleared his throat and picked out his brother-in-law from the sea of faces. Jack glared at him and snarled, "It's because of you that I am here!"

Then he spoke the words that the crowd would never forget: "I am an innocent man. And as long as my name is tainted, no grass shall grow upon my grave."

The sheriff stepped up and placed a black hood over Jack's head, but Jack cried, "Let us see again!"

The sheriff pulled the hood off. Jack looked all around. Then the hood was lowered again and the noose placed around his neck. People held their breath.

The signal was given. The trap door sprang open. The crowd gasped as Jack Mays plunged toward the ground. He fell six to eight feet before the rope snapped tight. His body jerked to a halt. There were more gasps and cries from the crowd as his twitching body swung back and forth. Five minutes later, Mays was declared dead.

The crowd drifted away. The body was removed and the scaffold torn down. Later a bank was built on the site.

Jack Mays had been a farmer. He was the choir leader at Rocky Ford Baptist Church. The crime that brought him to his end occurred on the night of June 17, 1898. Martha Higgins, the wealthy widow of a veteran of the War of 1812, was found dead in the remains of her home. She'd been struck on the head, and the home had been set on fire. Legend says the fire began when the killer ignited an oil cloth thrown over the body.

Mays had known Higgins and was an immediate suspect, but he had an alibi. He claimed to have been in Virginia, selling horses for the widow, at the time of the murder. When arrested he had on him a large sum of money. A few days later an empty trunk that had belonged to Martha Higgins was found in the Mitchell River.

The small community of Devotion was divided from the

start. Some believed Jack's claim of innocence. Others, including his brother-in-law, pronounced him guilty.

Shadrach C. Franklin, the best attorney in Surry County, defended Jack. The prosecution, contending that Mays killed Martha Higgins, took the trunk, stole the money, and disposed of the trunk in the river, sought the death penalty due to the heinous nature of the crime.

Though his alibi appeared to check out, Mays was convicted. The judge sentenced him to "hang by the neck until dead."

In those days there were no lengthy or automatic appeals. Executions were often carried out very swiftly after trials. It isn't clear whether Franklin appealed his client's conviction, but if he did, he lost. Jack Mays met his death on the gallows five months after Martha Higgins' murder.

The pious members of Rocky Ford Baptist Church refused to allow Mays' burial in their cemetery. Instead his remains were interred on his farm which was behind the church.

The brother-in-law that Mays had accused lived on. Legend says that on his deathbed this brother-in-law confessed that he, and not Jack Mays, killed Martha Higgins. However Mays was never officially cleared of the crime.

Jack's words from the brink of the abyss proved prophetic. To this day, no grass grows on his grave. Only a few meager weeds cover Mays' final resting place. It is an eerie, lonesome grave, and some visitors say they can feel the despairing soul there, unable to rest.

Apparently Martha Higgins doesn't rest either. The frame of her old home place stands yet, perched on its lonely hill. Some summer nights, people claim you can see a strange, otherworldly glow emanating from what had been the second floor—the reenactment of Martha's gruesome end.

Was Jack Mays innocent or guilty? The evidence against him was obviously flimsy and circumstantial. There is an anecdote about the execution that says the sheriff quietly asked Mays if he were guilty or innocent just before the trap door opened. If he answered innocent, the sheriff had a pardon from the governor. Mays answered, "I am guilty."

There is no mention of such a conversation in the well-known taped account of the hanging by Joseph Sanford Brown. And there is no record of the pardon.

Whatever the truth was, neither Jack Mays nor Martha Higgins are yet satisfied.

The Legends of East Hall

East Hall, Appalachian State University, Boone
Watauga County

One of the oldest buildings on the Appalachian State University is East Residence Hall. It's also the most haunted.

There are tens of dozens of ghost stories concerning this "C" shaped building. I lived in East for three and one-half years and worked there for two years as an office assistant in the Work-Study Program. I heard many strange stories from the residents and experienced some eerie moments myself. Here are two of them:

.

The Ghost(s) in the Dungeon

The most widely known of East Residence Hall's ghost stories concerns a young man who lived on the level called Subfloor. That level, located between the basement and the first floor, gets its name because one end is underground. East Hall is built on sloping land.

The tall, dark-haired young man who lived on Subfloor kept to himself. He grew depressed and decided to take his own life. One evening he entered the basement through the doors nearest Lovill Hall, climbed the stairs, went into his bedroom, and killed himself, either with a gun or a noose. Word of the student's death buzzed around campus and was reported by the local newspapers. It was the first reported suicide since Appalachian became a full university.

Before the suicide, a story already existed of a ghost in East Hall's basement, or "Dungeon." The shade of a forlorn young man or woman, who had killed him\herself in a women's bathroom, showed itself in the Dungeon and on Subfloor. That bathroom is creepy. One feels smothered in its limited space. Many people refuse to use it, and those who do report feeling they aren't alone or that they're being watched. Footsteps, voices, and tapping have all been heard in the Dungeon.

Over the years the story of the earlier ghost and of the young man who committed suicide became intertwined.

During the fall semester of 1987, James, a resident on Subfloor, personally encountered the specter.

One night James stood in the hall of Subfloor, talking with several other guys. A young man none of them recognized came around the corner and walked toward them. He was tall and unshaven, with dark hair, and wore jeans and a plaid shirt. The young man passed the group without speaking, opened the door to a room, went in, and closed the door behind him.

James and the group in the hall kept talking until one boy remembered the occupants of the room the unknown young man had entered weren't home. Their suspicions mounted. They decided to check it out.

One knocked on the door. No answer. The boys waited and listened. Not a sound came from the room. They opened the door, flipped on the light, and entered. No one was there.

The boys opened the sliding doors and looked in the closets. They checked under the beds. They found the windows locked, with the screens still in place. There was no one in the room. James and his friends looked at each other and quickly left.

This incident created a buzz in the dorm.

When Halloween came a few weeks later, East Hall held its annual "Dorm of Doom" spook trail. James set up his sound system in a classroom in the Dungeon. At the end of the night, he was the last one remaining as he gathered his equipment.

James heard the outer doors open and slam. Odd, he thought, they're supposed to be chained shut. He was kneeling by the classroom door and he looked up as footsteps approached. A young man appeared in the doorway. From the dark hair, unshaven face, and clothing, James recognized him as the visitor from a few weeks earlier. The young man passed the doorway.

James dove into the hallway, landing on his side. He looked both directions, but the hall was empty, even though he still heard footsteps heading toward the stairs.

Sure enough, the outer door was chained shut.

The ghost appeared again in the fall of 1991. A group of more than a dozen students had heard the story and decided to check it out. They went down one night to the Dungeon and entered what later became the lobby of the Watauga College offices.

The group stood there, talking. Suddenly a shadowy figure appeared in their midst. The students ran for the stairs, having all become believers in ghosts.

The ghost has been seen many other times. The most eerie incident occurred when some items were found behind a vent grill in the main Dungeon classroom: the items were an old tennis shoe and a yellowed newspaper with the account of the young man's suicide.

The ghost(s) in the Dungeon may walk the halls forever, retracing their last mortal movements.

The Towel

This incident has become an enduring anecdote of East Hall ghost lore. It shows a playful side of the spooks that infest the old dorm. The incident occurred on December 8, 1988, on 2nd Main and the men's shower room on 2nd New.

I lived on the coed 2nd Main. The only big bathroom on our hall was reserved for women, so we men had to walk all the way around to 2nd New.

One of the residents, let's call him Rob, always kept a big towel and a face cloth on the towel rack in his room. His were distinctive because of his initials in the corner. Around 8 a.m. one morning, Rob put on his sweats, grabbed his towel and toiletries, and left his room to go take a shower.

Ten minutes later Rob returned. His roommate Mike looked up from studying and saw Rob standing with the towel wrapped about his waist.

"Man," Mike said, "you're dripping all over the floor!"

"Well, it was really creepy," Rob answered. "I took my shower, but the whole time I felt like I was being watched!"

Mike laughed. "It's those ghost stories they've been telling."

"Maybe." Rob didn't think he'd imagined it. He dried off and got dressed. He went over to the sink and hung his towel on his rack. Mike looked up and saw him hang his towel.

Rob brushed his teeth while Mike studied. A few seconds later Rob cried out. Something about the way he yelled made Mike get up and walk to the sink area. He found Rob with a pale face and wide eyes. "What's up?" Mike asked, but he saw before Rob could answer.

The towel rack was empty.

Had someone reached in and taken it? No. The door was shut tight. No one could open their door without it giving off a loud, distinctive squeak.

The boys looked all around. All of Rob's other towels were in his closet, neatly stacked and dry, but the one he'd used that morning had simply vanished. The boys gave up finding it.

Mike had to get ready for class, so he walked over to the bathroom. He entered, shocked to find it freezing. He could see his breath. The heat came out full blast as it always did, but for some reason the bathroom felt like it wasn't heated that morning.

As Mike approached the showers, he saw a towel hanging on an empty stall. He stopped dead. A chill shot up his spine.

The towel had Rob's initials on it.

Mike grabbed the towel and ran back to his room. He showed Rob. They confirmed that each of them had seen that Rob hadn't returned to the room naked.

Both boys skipped classes that day. It would be months before they could tell anyone what happened.

These are just a couple of the ghost stories concerning East Hall. They range from benign and playful to downright scary. What makes East so active? Is it simply because it's an old building with a long history? Does something draw spirits to this place? Or are people just more open to such things there? Only the ghosts know the answer, and they won't tell.

The Legend of Greer Hall

I. G. Greer Hall, Appalachian State University, Boone
Watauga County

I. G. Greer Hall sits on the east side of the Appalachian State campus. It is the home of the Philosophy and Religion Departments and the College of Arts and Sciences. Greer was once the music building, and from this past, a ghostly legend has filled its halls for more than three decades.

In the big auditorium where an organization known as APPS provides movies for the students, music recitals were once held. During one of those recitals, a certain talented young woman was scheduled to play. Her boyfriend, a former student, had promised to return to Boone that night to hear the recital, just as he always did. He always sat in the same seat, located in the middle of the balcony. The seat had a loud, resounding squeak, which had become their signal that he had arrived and was ready to hear her play.

The young woman felt nervous that night that someone else might sit there, so she asked a friend to sit alongside and save her boyfriend's seat.

The recital started while the woman waited backstage to hear the familiar squeak. She waited and waited. Her time came to play, but she asked others to go ahead of her and let her wait for her boyfriend. This was to be her final recital, and she knew he wouldn't let her down by missing it.

The recital drew near its end. Where was he? She couldn't wait much longer.

Then she heard the squeak.

A wave of relief swept over her. She went out on stage and gave her best performance ever. When she finished, she stood and bowed.

Something was wrong. Through the loud applause from the audience, she couldn't hear her boyfriend whistling like he always did. She walked off the stage to learn the truth, and then her world shattered. Her boyfriend hadn't been there; he would never again come to her. He had died in a terrible automobile accident that night as he hurried toward Boone.

But what about the seat's squeak? Her friend insisted the seat had fallen open by itself, and stayed open, though empty, the whole time.

After that night people heard strange noises in the auditorium, like footsteps, eerie voices, and bumps. The noises came from the balcony. The seat with the distinctive squeak was heard opening again and again. At times the seat wouldn't stay closed.

Then the ghost showed himself. During at least two rehearsals in the auditorium the ghost appeared. Needless to say, the rehearsals were disrupted. Horrified professors recognized the dead boy. Some nights ghostly music floated across the evening air. People said the phantom was at it again.

Many have scoffed at this story, but a psychic researcher from the Rhyne Research Center at Duke University sensed a spectral presence in the building a few years ago. She wasn't familiar with the story at the time.

One night in April 1988, two APPS workers were in the building after the late showing of a film. They counted the money from the ticket and snack sales, then began to clean the auditorium. Suddenly piano music came from the main level below them. They thought someone had been locked inside. The young man and woman went down to the stage.

As they opened the door, one final note was struck on the piano, a note that hung in the air as the lights came on. The two workers couldn't believe they'd found an empty amphitheater. There was no way anyone could have hidden themselves so quickly.

Then from up in the theater above them came a series of thuds. The man and woman raced up the stairs, hearing the bumping even after they had entered the auditorium. No one else was there.

The two workers locked the doors and left the building. Outside they found a security officer and told him what they'd experienced. The officer led them back into Greer Hall.

In the lobby, the big portrait of I. G. Greer hung upside down. Strewn from one end of the lobby to the other was the paper money from the cash box. While the officer searched the building, the two workers picked up the money. Not one dollar was missing.

The workers rehung Greer's portrait upright, and the officer rejoined them, having found nothing. All three heard a thud and a snap from the balcony. They looked at each other. The officer cautiously led the workers up the steps.

One seat in the balcony's middle set was open. In it sat the trash bags the workers had been using. All three shook their heads, decided this was too much, and dashed down the stairs. The young man grabbed the cash box and headed for the door. The young woman paused to glance at the portrait of I. G. Greer. Once more it hung upside down.

The auditorium of Greer Hall has been refurbished, and the old seats replaced with plush, spring-loaded versions. The ghostly squeak echoes no more. However, many people say they still hear footsteps on the stairs. And the portrait of Greer still has a tendency to turn itself on end.

The Phantom of Howard Knob

Boone
Watauga County

Howard Knob, commonly known as Howard's Knob, is the great colossus that rises over downtown Boone. The knob takes its name from Benjamin Howard, who allegedly hid there from authorities in the 1770s. Large summer homes dot the mountain. A county park surrounds the knob, where a giant windmill, a failed experiment in power production, once stood. Howard Knob is a popular getaway for Appalachian State University and Watauga High School students, since it provides a great view of the Appalachian campus and the city of Boone.

The park is locked at night, and trespassers run afoul of the law. Some students take the risk in order to catch the night view of shimmering lights below. However, a few people have encountered something that made them never go back, even in daylight. They claim a phantom roams the knob.

On that night several years ago, three carloads of kids ventured up the mountain. They climbed over the park gate. The night was dark, but some of the kids had flashlights.

They were rewarded with the fantastic view of the city lights. The group dispersed as some wandered off, but they all agreed to meet back at the clearing around eleven o'clock. The kids that stayed at the clearing sat in a circle and told ghost stories.

At eleven, the rest of the group returned. Some were surprised the police hadn't shown up yet to run them off. The wind, which always blows up on the knob, grew stronger. The stars began to vanish, and all the students knew a storm approached.

As a cold rain began to fall the group started to leave, but one of the girls suddenly screamed. Others responded with startled cries.

A boy yelled, "What is it?"

The girl who had screamed couldn't answer. Her mouth hung open, her eyes stretched wide. She pointed a trembling finger at the crest of the hill. Every eye in the group followed her pointing finger.

A tall figure stood by a tree. In one hand he held a lantern that projected an eerie, sickly glow. His other hand held a pitchfork. He wore a long, black robe, with a hood pulled over his head that left only a dark spot where his face should have been. He thrust the pitchfork toward the gate.

None of the group moved. They couldn't. The figure shook the pitchfork angrily and took a menacing step forward. Some of the kids swore two red eyes glowered out from inside the hood.

Now the group moved as if one. Screams filled the night air, punctured only by the sound of scrambling feet. Some jumped over the gate, some went under, and not one dared to look back in case the ghostly thing might be right behind them. The last kid barely made it into the car before all three drivers floored their accelerators, making tires spin dirt and gravel.

To this day not one of the group that saw that figure has been back to Howard Knob.

What did they see? A prank? Someone scaring away trespassers? Or was it something else? The phantom has been seen at other times. No one has had the courage to get close enough to see who or what could be the phantom of Howard Knob. Maybe we don't really want to know.

Flat Top Manor:
Moses Cone's Getaway

Blue Ridge Parkway, Blowing Rock
Watauga County

On the ridge of Flat Top Mountain, a great white monolith peers out across the valley. The distant trout lake glistens in the sunlight and reflects the glow of the moon. Standing on the front porch of Flat Top Manor, one can almost feel the passage of history.

Rumors of ghosts haunting the old manor have abounded for years. Officially, staff members say the stories are not true, that they were created to stir interest. Privately, however, some conceded that many unexplained incidents have indeed occurred.

Moses H. Cone, known as "the Denim King" because of the heavy duty, deep blue denim his textile mills produced, built his twenty-room palace at the turn of the century as a getaway for his family and friends and as a spot to entertain political figures. His was a fascinating world. The last Tsar reigned in Russia, and Kaiser Wilhelm II began to build up the German navy, an act that alarmed other countries and helped bring on the first

World War. The United States was not yet a true world power. Especially in the South, the country slowly recovered from the Civil War.

Cone had fallen in love with the mountain region and bought up land around Blowing Rock. When he built his home, he employed many of the same people whose land he had bought, allowing them to remain in their homes. Cone and his wife, Bertha, were early conservationists and planted many trees such as apple, serviceberry, cherry, oak, hickory, birch, and white pine. They imported sugar maples from New England which flourished in the cool, misty mountain air. Moses also became involved in the growing town of Blowing Rock, helping the local schools by giving them "four dollars for every one dollar raised by the citizens of the town." He also gave money to what would become Appalachian State University and served on the school's original board.

Cone didn't get to enjoy his summer palace for long. He died in 1908 at the age of 51. His widow used the manor for many years although not for the lively parties her husband intended. Bertha often strolled, brooding, around the "Widow's Walk" atop the house. She apparently never got over the passing of her husband. When she died in 1947, she donated the estate to Greensboro's Moses Cone Memorial Hospital, which gave the manor and 3,500 acres to the United States government in 1950.

Today the Cone property is a national park, and the manor house serves as a gift shop and craft center. People come to ride horses, walk the 25 miles of beautiful carriage trails that Moses built for Bertha, or just sit on the front porch and take in the view.

The tourists and the staff may not be the only ones there. Late at night people have seen the restless specter of Bertha Cone, staring out a window and strolling about the Widow's

Walk. There is a story that she may have wanted the manor house boarded up. Her spirit may be unhappy with the public going through her home. According to one story, she had fought to keep the National Park Service from building the Blue Ridge Parkway through her estate.

Another shade has been seen at Flat Top Manor, that of a beautiful young girl often referred to as "Clementine." Some say she was the Cones' daughter, but they had no children. Perhaps she was the child of a relative or friend, or maybe she was there before the Cones arrived. Whatever her origins, the child's lonely shade has appeared on the stairs, the closed-off second floor, and in the attic. Most often she stands in a doorway, or visitors have glimpsed her from the corners of their eyes.

Caretakers used to live on the second floor. They saw apparitions on several occasions and experienced eerie things like unexplained bumps, mysterious lights, ghostly footsteps, and haunting music. Objects disappeared from their spots, only to reappear later in the place they'd originally been left. On one occasion, the family heard noises on the floor above them. As they listened, they heard the unmistakable sound of furniture being moved. The problem was that no one but the caretakers was in the house at the time. They waited until the noises stopped before they went up to investigate. They found, in the heavy dust on the floor, marks that indicated furniture had definitely been moved. However, the only footprints they found were their own.

Another time, while the rest of his family was away, the caretaker decided it would be a good day to deal with the bugs and mice that infested the manor. He contacted an exterminator, who sent out two men. With the caretaker's help, they made their way through the house. When they reached a certain swinging door, the men pushed, but the door wouldn't budge. It felt like someone was holding it from the other side.

No, that couldn't be, they decided; the door must just be jammed. All three men gave a mighty heave. The door gave just a little, but wouldn't open. So they pulled. The resistance finally let go and the door opened. The three men walked through the door, just in time to see another door on the other side of the room swing wildly as though someone had run through it.

The caretaker soon took his family and left.

A few years ago a couple from Appalachian State University visited Flat Top Manor at night to see if there were any ghosts around. He was a devout skeptic and vowed to prove there were no such things as ghosts. So they drove to the manor and walked around the grounds. They looked around the house, into the windows, and then went to the Carriage House. With no moon, the night hung black around them, but nothing happened other than the wind began to blow.

They started back toward the house. The boy haughtily said, "See, no ghost!"

The girl opened her mouth to reply, but never got the chance. A blood-curdling, mournful scream shrilled past them and into the valley. She stared into the darkness, feeling every muscle in her body tensing to explode. A chill came over the girl like she'd never felt. As the shriek died away, she reached for her boyfriend.

He bolted, leaving her alone on the dark trail. She ran after him, praying that nothing followed her. She reached the parking lot and heard keys jingling. "You'd better not leave me!" she screamed. She reached the car just as her boyfriend jammed it into gear. They left the park with squealing tires.

Neither was sure later what they'd heard. The girl gave other reasons for breaking up soon after, but her boyfriend almost leaving her that night had to have something to do with it.

Do unhappy phantoms roam the halls and pathways of Flat Top Manor? Was that scream the cry of a forlorn spirit? Does

Bertha Cone walk the Widow's Walk, forever mourning her lost husband and the life they planned together? And what of the child? Who is she? What keeps her tragic spirit attached to this place?

When you visit, be respectful, lest Bertha Cone take offense.

The Richmond Hill
Law School

Yadkin County

Judge Richmond M. Pearson built Richmond Hill in 1848, ten years before he would become North Carolina's Chief Justice. Pearson used his estate not only as his home, but also as a school of law. Nearly 1,000 students came from all over to study with the judge, who ran his school rather informally. He sometimes held classes under the trees outside. Pearson spent a lot of time with each individual and didn't mind giving an impromptu lecture when the opportunity arose. The law school flourished until Pearson's death in 1878.

Some students had boarded in the main house, while others lived in small cabins. There was also a classroom building. After the school closed, the Pearson heirs eventually sold the property. Several families lived in the mansion. Legend says the last family fled in terror after hearing an unseen presence on the stairs and seeing snakes crawl across the ceiling. The estate deteriorated. More strange stories developed.

In the 1940s, some hunters approached the property with

their dogs. As they reached the decayed house, the dogs grew uneasy. Every animal whimpered, tucked its tail, and scampered back into the woods. The hunters couldn't understand their dogs' behavior until the sensation came over each of them that someone or something watched them.

Other people claimed to hear strange sounds coming from the abandoned estate. Some heard soft, whispered voices. Others heard loud footsteps, roaming through the old house.

The few who ventured to Richmond Hill after dark claimed to have seen an eerie light on the right, second-floor window. When they turned away and then looked back, the light had disappeared.

The main house, the only building still standing, was eventually restored and placed on the National Register of Historic Places. A county park surrounds the structure. In 1991, the caretaker's wife, who took my friend Melanie and me on a tour of the house, said that people used to hear what sounded like rattling chains descending the stairway. She indicated she had never heard the chains and felt skeptical about the story.

Perhaps the voices, footsteps, and chains have disappeared, becoming only relics from the past. The light in the window is another matter.

Recently two girls drove down the winding, dirt road toward Richmond Hill. They could see by the beams of their headlights that the park was deserted. The girls had heard the story about the light in the second floor window. As they approached the house, sure enough, a strange light appeared.

The girl who drove said, "I thought it was our headlights, so I turned them off. But the light was still there. We turned around and got out of there. I looked over my shoulder and the light was gone!"

Does Judge Pearson still walk the halls of his beloved home? Or is there a student's spirit lurking about his beloved school?

Some say the noises and lights occurred even in Judge Pearson's time. Others say all the haunting stories were made up to keep people away. No one knows for sure what's behind the strange incidents at Richmond Hill.

A Sad History

Near Huntsville
Yadkin County

Yadkin County's most well-known "haunt" is a crumbling house in a town that died. Ghosts or not, the history of this old house is a tapestry of tragedy.

The house once stood as a towering, white sentinel, the hub of society in antebellum Huntsville, near the Shallow Ford of the Yadkin River. Politicians, military officers, and Southern "belles" graced the ornate rooms of the great mansion. A woman named Sarah and her daughter Julia moved into the house soon after its completion. Julia grew up happy there. She married a plaster worker named Henry, and they lived in the house with Sarah.

In 1854, Julia bore a son, Paul. The child was sickly. The parents doted on their boy, smothering him with love and hoping to improve his health. Paul could rarely go outside to play. He grew spoiled, but not healthier. He died in 1858.

Julia never accepted the death of her son. She took to searching through the house, or wandering through the woods, calling Paul's name. Around 1860 she actually began to see her precious child. She would stand for hours on the second-floor balcony overlooking their property, waiting until she could see him. "Paul, my son!" she'd wail.

Then one day as Julia stood on the balcony, she fell or jumped. Legend says there was a stake in the ground that was used to tie cows and horses. Julia landed on that stake and impaled herself. She died instantly.

Sarah continued to live in the house after her daughter's death. Her brother joined her, but happiness never found the family there.

After Sarah died, a doctor purchased the stately home. He moved in with his family, wife Mollie and daughter Daisy. Mother and daughter never got along. Daisy was fourteen years old in 1896 when her father died, leaving the women and Mollie's brother, Will, living in the house.

Mollie had no idea how to handle Daisy as the girl grew more distant and difficult. Mollie finally just gave up, so Daisy found attention elsewhere.

The family had a handyman also named Will. Daisy fell in love with him and an illicit affair began. In late summer or early fall 1901, Daisy found she was pregnant. Mollie's family flew into an uproar. These aristocrats of a long Southern line couldn't stand the embarrassment of a scandal. They'd founded the nearby town. And now an affair with the hired help? And pregnant! Tempers turned ugly.

On a cold winter day, the coldest anyone could remember, Will the handyman was found lying in the snow close to town. He'd been shot dead. The ground was so frozen the body had to be pried up with a shovel.

Most versions of the murder say that Daisy saw her lover gunned down, either by her mother, her uncle Will, or a hired killer. Authorities charged Uncle Will with the murder, but the case never went to trial. Will moved west.

The trauma scarred Daisy. She was never the same. When her child was born in either February or April, 1902, he came out prematurely and scarred too. The boy, named Jack, had no sweat glands. This made his skin appear scaly, like a fish. Though he didn't go into public very often, those who saw him gasped. He was an intriguing and frightening sight. Jack became cruelly known as "fishboy" and later "fishman."

He could never play with the other children; they made fun of him. Jack was taught at home and grew up educated and well-mannered. His demeanor was usually pleasant enough, and those who looked beyond his appearance knew immediately that he came from gentry.

In later years, misunderstanding and frustration got to Jack. He served ten years in prison for arson. In 1964, he was arrested in a shooting, but the charges were dropped. Jack spent his last years in a small house along the Yadkin River. In 1972, at the age of seventy, Jack died. His remains were interred at a nearby Baptist church.

Ghost stories about the house go back more than a century. People used to say they caught glimpses of little Paul, romping about the yard he'd barely seen in life. Many claimed to hear Julia's ethereal voice, calling out to her lost son. Some saw her standing on the balcony, her tense, lonely face peering across the landscape in search of Paul. One or two people heard the scream of her death plunge.

Another legend sprang up earlier this century, but has faded. Several people claimed on cold, snowy days that they heard Daisy's desperate cry of "Noooo!" just before a gunshot.

Jack's spirit has been seen a few times, lurking in the woods near his old home, or along the banks of the river. People who live near the old house now say they've never seen or heard anything. The owner lived there for years and never experienced any kind of spooky activity. The house, once a lustrous white, is now dingy, and one of the chimneys is crumbling at the top. The steps to the front porch collapsed. A mobile home sits in the yard near the house.

The town of Huntsville once thrived and was even a candidate to become state capital. Instead it disappeared. The old house stands as a reminder of a time lost. Maybe those who lived and died there have finally found peace.

Ghost Lights on Brown Mountain

Avery, Burke, Caldwell, and Watauga counties

Viewing Spots:
Lost Cove Overlook, Blue Ridge Parkway
Brown Mountain Lights Pull-off, N.C. 181
Wiseman's View, off N.C. 181
Grandfather Mountain, Linville, North Carolina

The Brown Mountain Lights are one of the best-documented, unexplained phenomenon in North Carolina. People have traveled from all over the world to see them. Scientists have tried unsuccessfully to find a natural explanation. No one knows for sure what they are, but one thing is certain: the lights are real.

There are many tales about the origins of the lights. The most common story originates in the 1850s. A man murdered his young wife and their child, then buried their remains in a hidden grave on remote Brown Mountain. When searchers later went looking for the bodies, a mysterious light guided them to the grave. Though a good story, this can't be the origin of the lights because they'd been seen much earlier.

Another popular legend, which became a bluegrass song, was of a devoted slave whose master disappeared on the mountain. The slave spent days and nights searching but couldn't find his master. Supposedly his ghost is still looking. The lights were seen earlier than this tale too.

The first documented sighting by white men came in 1771. A German engineer surveying the area reported seeing "strange lights" on the distant ridge.

Native Americans who lived in the region had seen the lights for centuries before that, back as far as 1200 A.D. Cherokee legends tell of a fierce battle between two warring tribes that took place on and around the low ridge of Brown Mountain. Hundreds of brave warriors died there. When their loved ones didn't return, the women searched for their bodies by torch light. Shortly thereafter, the lights began to appear.

Over the years many explanations for the lights have been given. Some have said they are caused by swamp gas; there's not a swamp for miles around. Others said the lights are reflections on the clouds. The fallacy there is that the lights usually don't show up when it's very cloudy.

One scientist carefully studied the problem and pronounced the lights were produced by the angle of the N.C. 181 overlook. He decided, "One is actually looking down, beyond the mountain, seeing streetlights, car lights, and train lights." The problem with this theory is obvious: in 1771 there were no towns in that area with street lights, not to mention cars or trains.

In 1916 and again in 1940, major floods swept through Western North Carolina. Roads and railways were washed out, and power was out for long periods. The lights still did their thing, oblivious to the natural disasters around them.

Some of the Brown Mountain Lights just flash and are gone as quickly as they came. Others remain a while. They glide along the ridge, or rise into the sky and wink out. The lights appear irregularly, randomly, shimmering and disappearing. Sometimes there is only one, while other times several appear at once. Some people have reported seeing ten or more at the same time.

The best time to see the lights is on a clear, dark, moonless night. Around 10 p.m. is usually a good viewing time, although the lights do often show up earlier. Some people say it's best to see the lights in the summer months, but they can be viewed year round. They've been spotted in every month.

If the weather is rainy, or cloudy, the lights will disappoint you and not show, or appear sporadically. At other times they'll dazzle you.

Ancient Native American ghosts? Murdered spirits? A faithful servant? Alien spaceships? Whatever they are, the Brown Mountain Lights continue to mesmerize and mystify.

The Devil's Cave

Richmond Hill Community
Yadkin County

An old dirt road meanders through the woods from Limerock Road, off Richmond Hill Church Road, down to the banks of the Yadkin River. The farther you go, the rougher the road becomes. At the river's bank rises a massive rock formation known as the Limerock.

Once a quarry, a great chunk of rock has been eaten out of the side of the ancient ridge. The quarry floor is a mess of mulch, mud, and stagnant water. A half-circle of sheer rock cliffs rise one hundred feet or more above the old road. On the backside of the great Limerock sits a dark, foreboding recess, the Devil's Cave.

No one is exactly sure who named the cave. Stories about it stretch back for centuries. The Indians who once roamed these woods claimed an evil spirit haunted the place. The German, Scots-Irish, and English settlers who moved in heard these stories, and its reputation grew as a "haunt." Some said the Devil himself could be found there, resting from his wanderings and mischief. Some claimed to hear mysterious groans and strange noises issuing from the cave's mouth that signaled Satan's presence.

In the 1920s or '30s, four teenage boys decided to challenge the legend. They armed themselves with two lanterns, a sling shot, and an old stick they used for baseball games and set out for the cave.

They reached the Limerock and found the cave. One boy remarked how quiet it was there. No animal noises. No wind rustling the trees. Even the lazy sound of the river was muted there. The boys looked at each other and tried not to show their fear. Each swore to himself he wouldn't be the one who ran first.

One by one they climbed into the cave. It was dark, cool, and damp, and smelled of rot and stagnant air. Their lanterns cast eerie shadows close by, but the lights didn't shine very far into the cave, as though the darkness was too thick to pass through.

One boy said, "What a smell! Whew!"

The darkness replied, "Whew!" All the boys jumped and screamed. Their screams came back from the darkness. Then they laughed.

A boy said, "An echo."

"An echo," returned from the back of the cave.

Another boy shouted a long greeting: "Heeeeey!"

"Heeeeey!"

The last boy howled like the wolfman: "A-hooooo!"

"A-hooooo!"

The boys all laughed, and the cave echoed that too. They grew more at ease and called out whatever they could think of, and their fun grew. Finally one boy yelled, "Come on out here if you're there ol' Devil, and fight like a man! I'll rip your horns out!"

The cave was silent.

The boys looked at each other, their laughter now gone. One

boy gulped and said, "You shouldn't have said that."

The echo growled, "You shouldn't have said that."

The boys trembled, fighting not to run away. From the darkness deep in the cave came a scraping sound. Like hooves on stone. Then they heard a series of grunts and growls. Two red dots appeared in the darkness—dots that glowed like eyes!

The boys forgot their pride and screamed with one voice. They dove for the cave's mouth, tumbled out and down into a heap of mud, then fought each other to get up and away. Once they started running, they didn't stop until they reached Hobson's farm, a few miles away.

One of the boys' hair turned white as snow within a few days.

Not one of the boys ever dared return to the Limerock.

Stories about the Devil's Cave came from other people, and the legend grew for years. Once the quarry was abandoned, fewer people went near the Limerock. The legend gradually faded. Older local residents still tell the tales; most people have forgotten them. But if you go near the Limerock and the Devil's Cave, it's best if you don't shout out any challenges.

"H-h-horse!"

East Bend
Yadkin County

A few days before Christmas 1929, a young boy named Billy went to the T. D. Smitherman Store in East Bend. He talked and laughed with other boys while the day passed. It was cold outside. Snow started falling, and it looked like it would be a white Christmas. Billy dreaded the chilly walk home, so he stayed at the store longer than he meant to. Dusk fell and still Billy lingered. Some of the other boys began telling ghost stories, and that finally made Billy leave because he didn't like ghost stories. The stories were about the woods he would pass through on his way home.

Billy made his way through the deepening darkness, trying to stay warm. An occasional snowflake drifted past. When Billy reached the woods on the eastern edge of town, it felt as though no one else was around for miles. He remembered a ghost story about the woods.

"Stop it," he said aloud. "You're just scaring yourself."

The sound of his voice steadied him a bit. He began to whistle as he moved into the woods. He didn't have that far to go before he'd be home. Then he heard something behind him.

Clop, clop, clop, clop.

Billy stopped, and the noise stopped.

He started moving again. Clop, clop, clop, clop.

No! Billy froze. His knees shivered, and not from the cold. His mouth fell open, his eyes couldn't stretch any wider. Billy's whole body shook. He decided no matter what, he would not turn around. He knew the story of these woods.

He started again, and behind him came the same clop. It had to be a horse's hooves striking the ground. Billy's heart pounded in his chest. He did the only thing possible. Run!

The hooves behind him ran. There was a snort and the sound of breathing. It seemed closer.

As he tried to run faster, Billy's foot caught a root. He sprawled onto the frozen ground.

The noise behind him stopped. Billy took a quick look back and found nothing there. He got up, brushed himself off, and felt better. His imagination had run wild with him. He said, "That was silly." He'd be home in a few minutes, and everything was okay. He bent over to rub a bruised knee.

Then he felt its presence. Slowly, so slowly, Billy lifted his eyes and looked behind him. This time it was there.

Not two feet away was a great, white stallion. The animal just stood there, close enough to nuzzle Billy, but it couldn't nuzzle him. It had no head. Its neck ended in a bloody stump.

Billy tried to scream, but no sound came from his mouth.

The horse took a step toward him.

Now Billy heard his own scream as he turned and ran.

The horse followed him. Billy felt it right behind him. He even felt hot breath spraying over his neck and head. That's impossible, his mind screamed. You have to have a head to breathe!

Billy burst from the woods onto the road. Surely he was safe now, but no, the horse came with him, running along the road right behind him. Billy ran like lightning.

Then the lights from his house came into view. Just a few yards more.

Billy slammed into the door, twisted the knob, and fell inside. His mother and father rushed toward him with startled yells as he threw the door shut.

"What is it, son?"

Billy struggled for breath. "H-h-horse!" Then the room spun and Billy fainted. His father looked out the window, but saw only falling snow.

This is just one of the many stories of the headless horse in East Bend. Many believe the origin may have been a tragic explosion during the American Revolution or Civil War.

The legend has faded somewhat over the years. A bypass of East Bend was built right through the area. The woods have thinned a lot, and several houses are there now. It looks a lot safer now than it did to Billy that dark night in 1929, but let any traveler on foot in that area beware. If you hear hooves behind you, don't look back.

The Doughboy

East Bend
Yadkin County

The year 1919 began more peacefully than had the previous year. True, civil war raged in Russia between the Reds and Whites, but the war which would later be known as World War I, the "war to end all wars," had ended in November of the previous year.

The American soldiers, called "doughboys," started coming home shortly after the armistice. They returned triumphantly to their wives, girlfriends, and families. Of course for some, the nation's victory came with deep sorrow; many brave young men never came home.

Thus was the case for one family in East Bend.

Just after they'd heard rumors that the war would soon be over, the news reached them. Their Johnny had been killed in France as his unit attempted to storm a German trench. His body had been irretrievable.

The young soldier's mother suffered a breakdown. The father tried to show his pride in his son's willingness to sacrifice everything for right and justice, but he couldn't hide his pain. And Johnny's younger brother, let's call him Jacob, simply refused to accept that his big brother wasn't coming home.

Weeks passed. Their lives went on. The mother recovered slowly, taking strength from her son's final words before he left: "Don't worry, Mom. No matter what, I'll always be with you."

Still Jacob held onto hope. It had to have been a mistake. His parents grew worried about their son. They told Jacob what the army had said, that Johnny's unit had been wiped out, but they couldn't bring themselves to crush the boy's faith.

One winter's day in early 1919, Jacob's friend Richard came over to play checkers. The weather was unsettled outside; the wind whipped, the clouds crossed the sky, growing darker. A thunderstorm began, and a cold rain blew. Richard decided to stay for supper and wait for the rain to let up.

The storm grew worse. Lightning lit up the deepening darkness, and thunder boomed around the house like artillery fire. The mother served the meal. Jacob said the blessing, asking as he always did for the return of his brother.

While the menfolk began eating, the mother walked around to the stove and picked up a pot of stew. She heard something outside, like a horse coming up the road, so she opened the curtains and looked out the window.

The night had turned dark. She saw the rain was heavy and now mixed with sleet. The lightning flashed, illuminating a horse and its rider. The mother dropped the pot of stew. It crashed on the floor, but she didn't care. Her hands covered her mouth. She gasped, "Dearest God!"

Her husband rushed over. "What is it?" He looked out, and his mouth dropped open.

Jacob and Richard crowded under the adults and peeked out the window. Jacob's face lit up. "It's Johnny! It's Johnny! See, I told ya he'd come home!"

The father held his head. "Is it possible?" He hugged his wife, and they cried, holding onto each other. Out in the yard, Johnny dismounted, opened the barn door, and led the animal inside.

Jacob yelled, "I'm going to meet him!"

The father said, "Yeah, go ahead. Wait, we'll all go! No, it's sleeting out there. Get your coat." He wiped his eyes and took a deep breath. "Wait. I'll go. I'll take his horse and send him on in here."

With shaking hands, the father pulled on his heavy coat. He ran out through the door. Minutes passed. "Where is he?" Jacob yelled, watching from the window. Finally the father returned.

"Where's Johnny?"

The father's face was pale. He shook his head. "I . . . I don't know." He pointed outside. His lips moved, but nothing came out.

Jacob yelled, "What? Where is he?"

The father swallowed. "He ain't in the barn. And there ain't no horse." His voice quivered. "And the only tracks out there are Richard's."

Mother hung her head and cried.

Jacob couldn't understand, so his father let him go look for himself. Only when he found nothing did he believe that Johnny hadn't come home. He joined his mother and father in crying.

Richard felt like he understood what had happened. The family all wanted to see Johnny so much that their minds had played a collective trick. True, he'd seen the figure on horseback too, but he'd been caught up in the joy of the moment.

The sleet turned to snow, so Richard stayed overnight. The mother and father slumped off to their bedroom, but Richard and Jacob stayed up late, talking about what they'd seen. Jacob finally went, tearfully, off to bed. Richard made himself a pallet of two blankets, close to the roaring fireplace and soon fell asleep.

When he awoke the room was dark. The fire had burned down until only orange embers remained. Richard decided to get up and put more wood in the fireplace, but then he realized he wasn't alone in the room. He couldn't see anyone, but he knew someone was there. He could feel a presence. But who was it?

Suddenly flames leaped out of the embers. The fire had come back to life. And standing before the fireplace, right beside Richard, was Jacob's brother. He held his arms toward the fire, warming himself.

Richard almost ran in panic until he realized who it was. This time there was no mistake, so he relaxed. He saw Johnny's face clearly in the firelight, saw his peaceful expression. Saw his uniform. Then Richard saw how tattered the uniform was. He saw the bullet holes.

Richard couldn't move. He didn't know what to do, so he waited, watching in horrified wonder. The flames burned down, then sparked again.

The doughboy was gone.

Now Richard moved. He searched the house, checked for a way into or out of the house, and found no one but the mother, father, and Jacob. Richard stoked the fire, then went into Jacob's room.

Jacob awoke at dawn, finding his friend sitting in an old rocking chair, not having slept. Jacob asked him what was wrong, but Richard quietly gathered his things and left. He didn't tell anyone what had happened for many years.

Today the house is gone, replaced by a church softball field. The East Bend Fair was held there for years.

The doughboy was never seen again after that night in 1919, when he made it home one last time to see the family he loved.

The Cox Place

Lone Hickory Road, South Oak Ridge Community
Yadkin County

The home of my Great-grandfather Charles Renegar once stood on Lone Hickory Road, just opposite the South Oak Ridge Baptist Church cemetery. My Grandfather George, my Great-aunt Nat Canter, and their siblings grew up in this cozy home.

Lone Hickory Road, which snakes its way from U.S. 601, south of Yadkinville, west to U.S. 21, was part of the Old Coach Road, or Old Wagon Road, that used to be a connector with Winston and Salem. On this lonely stretch was the Cox place. No house had been on the property in living memory, but there was an old abandoned graveyard in the woods. Supposedly African-Americans were buried there during those years of slavery and segregation. No headstones stood there, but the graves were obvious because they had sunk in. An open well stood nearby, one that everyone assumed had served the house that no one could remember.

When Aunt Nat was born in 1908, the tales of the Cox light were already legend. The phenomenon frequently occurred.

When Nat was a little girl, the family tended tobacco in a barn in the woods just west of the house. When tobacco was curing, several people would sleep under the sheltered eave at the front of the barn. One night, Nat couldn't sleep. She sat up and looked through the trees. She clearly saw the Cox light. It rose from where she knew the open well to be, moved around the road, and then swept over the hidden graveyard.

Frightened, Nat tried to wake her father. Charles grumbled and rolled over. Nat turned around and saw that the light was still there. His sister's commotion woke George, and he got up to see what was happening. He was startled and called, "Pap, get up. 'Tis a light!" This time Charles got up, dressed, grabbed his rifle, and went off towards the Cox place. George trailed him, pulling on his boots as he stumbled along. They followed the light, but no matter how they tried, they couldn't get near it. They gave up, realizing they'd encountered the Cox ghost light.

Many others saw the light, either hovering over the old well, moving in the cemetery, or along the road. No one could get near it. No one could ever explain the light, or the way it roamed. It stayed there for years, but finally faded from memory. Someone filled in the old well.

Aunt Nat always thought that maybe, long years ago, someone stumbled upon the open well at night, fell in, and drowned. Maybe the Cox light was the spirit of the unknown victim, trying to let somebody know where he/she had died. With the well filled in, that poor spirit's remains are lost forever.

More than a quarter of a century has passed since the light was last seen, but if you happen to drive down Lone Hickory Road at night, keep an eye open.

Taking Mary Home

Yadkin County

The young woman struggled up the bank, fighting the slope, the rain, the mud, and her soaked ballroom gown, all at the same time. She could see the lights of passing cars from the road above. Her mind was consumed with one thought: to get home and let Mama know she was all right.

Finally, she reached the top of the embankment and stood beside the road. She brushed the hair out of her eyes with one hand and waved the other frantically at an approaching car.

She was afraid the driver wouldn't see her for the driving rain, but he did. The car slowed to a stop in front of the soaked teenager. Inside was an older couple.

The woman rolled down her window and exclaimed, "My goodness, child, what's happened?"

"There's been an accident, but I'm all right," the girl replied. "I just need a ride."

"Get in back there, honey," the old woman told her. "We'll take you wherever you need to go."

"Thank you," the relieved girl said as she opened the back door and climbed inside.

She looked around as she closed the door, and the old man drove on. This vehicle was strange; bigger than any she had ever seen. She settled into the soft, plush seat, feeling guilty for the puddles of water forming on the seat and in the floorboard.

"I'm getting your beautiful car all wet," she said softly.

"That's all right, dear," the old woman said. "What's your name?"

"My name is Mary," the girl replied. "Oh please, won't you take me home?"

"No problem," the old man said. Funny, thought Mary, he sounds so distant and hollow; almost like he was far away. As she listened to the old couple talk to each other, she realized that they both sounded strange. She shook her head. Maybe she just had water in her ears.

They drove along for a little while, and Mary did her best to answer the elderly pair's questions, but mostly she just sat in silence. She was only concerned with making sure her Mama knew she was okay.

Suddenly, Mary grew excited—they were approaching her home. "There!" she cried. "That driveway!"

Mary's heart swelled with joy as the old man slowed down and turned into her driveway. The girl was on the edge of her seat. She smiled when she saw the light on the front porch was glowing. Mama was waiting up for her! She giggled with delight. She'd made it!

Then her joyful heart was stricken with a sudden jolt. Mary was overwhelmed by a violent seizure. Her vision began to cloud. "No!" she moaned. "Not again!" Then there was darkness. The old couple had not heard her despairing moan of protest. "Here you are, dear," the old woman said as she turned around. Mary wasn't there.

"Mary?" the lady called, confused. "Herb, where'd she go?"

"Beats me, Margaret," her husband replied. "Maybe she jumped out!"

Margaret didn't think so. She joined her husband as he got out and went up to the house. As they stepped up on the porch, the front door opened. A very old woman, even older than they were, opened the door. She regarded the visitors with a look of sad resignation.

"Ma'am," Herb told her, "we picked up a young lady a little ways down the road who said she lives here. Seems she's took off, though."

The older woman sighed. "Yes, I've been expecting you for a while now."

"What?" Margaret said in surprise. "But . . . we don't even know you . . . or that young woman!"

"I know," the lady in the doorway said sadly, brushing aside a tear. "The girl you picked up was our daughter, Mary. This happens every year, on this same night, but she never gets here."

Herb was deeply disturbed by now. "What happens?" he demanded.

Mary's mother shook her head. "Twenty-five years ago, this very night, our darling Mary lost her life in a wreck where you picked her up. The car went airborne and hit a tree. She died instantly."

"What are you saying?" Margaret gasped, her face pale.

The woman gave her a sad little smile and said, "Thank you for your kindness and the trouble you took to drive up here. But, you see, yours is the twenty-fifth car that's been here, bringing Mary home."

Then the woman shut the door, leaving Herb and Margaret staring at each other. Slowly, they turned to look at their empty car.

This story is one of the oldest of the so-called "vanishing hitchhiker" stories. The accident, still recalled by those who heard about it as youngsters, occurred somewhere in western Yadkin County on or near U.S. 21, sometime in the 1910s or 1920s. Mary's boyfriend was also killed, but hasn't been sighted. The tree they struck stands there still, an ugly scar remaining near the top of the trunk. The road Mary lived on has been named in her honor.

Sightings of Mary stopped a couple of decades ago when her mother finally died. The house stands empty now. It seems Mary and her mother were reunited at last. Hopefully, they have both found peace, somewhere over Jordan.

Willie Meets the Spook

The Haunted Railroad Bridge, Statesville
Iredell County

Willie was nervous. He looked around constantly as he walked down the lonely old rail line. It was a hot night, and high clouds covered the moon. There was just enough light for him to see where he was going.

Willie was really jumpy. He didn't like to be out this late at night, especially by himself. But he had to get home. His senses were on high alert, ready for any animal, or worse, a highwayman, to jump out of the bushes.

The silence hanging in the night air was suddenly pierced by the bone-chilling shriek of a screech owl. Willie froze, his hair standing on end. His great-grandmother, a deeply superstitious woman, had told Willie as a child that screech owls were "harbingers," foretelling something about to take place. This only heightened Willie's anxiety.

Willie really had no need to fear any man. The six-foot-four, 230-pound, thirty-nine-year-old descendant of former slaves was as strong as a horse. What scared Willie was the thought

83

of "spooks." He'd grown up with tales of "boogers," the loupga-rou, monsters, zombies, and ghosts, told by various members of his large family. A shudder ran through Willie as he recalled some of those scary tales. Ahead, Willie could see that he was approaching a railway bridge. He gulped. Bostian's bridge!

He'd almost forgotten about having to cross the old span. He really didn't want to do it, but it would take too long now for him to go back and take another route home.

There was a ghost story associated with this stretch of rail and the bridge, and Willie remembered it all too well. On August 27, 1891, Passenger Train Number Nine, bound from Salisbury to Asheville, had met a horrible fate here. At around 3 a.m. that morning, the train approached Bostian's bridge. It derailed off the bridge, plunging ninety feet to the ravine below. Thirty people were killed and dozens upon dozens were injured.

One of those killed was H. K. Linster, the train's baggage master. Many people claimed that Linster's ghost would appear quite often, asking the correct time in order to set his watch. Linster was due to retire after working for the railroad for thirty years and had been given the watch as a retirement present. He brought it out often, hoping people would see it.

All of a sudden, Willie realized that today was August 27th. He'd heard that every year, on the anniversary of the tragic wreck, the whole horrible scene was repeated. No one ever saw the train, but they did hear it approaching. Then the awful sounds of the crash, the rupturing of steam pipes, the collision of the metal cars and hard earth, and finally, the awful screams of the victims.

Willie broke out in a cold sweat. What time was it anyway? He'd left his sister's house long after midnight. He began to tremble as he realized that it had to be nearly 3 a.m.

He composed himself, shaking it off. That was just an old spook tale. There weren't any such things as ghosts... were there?

A strange calm settled over the man as he started to cross the bridge. Halfway across, his confidence began to grow. He smiled and sighed with relief. It was just an old tale after all. Finally, after a seeming eternity, he stepped off the end of the bridge. The man laughed out loud at himself. He couldn't believe he'd let the old legend scare him so.

Then he heard it. The laughter died on his lips and his mouth suddenly went dry. There was a low, steady rumble. It seemed to be getting closer and closer, approaching from the east, in front of him.

Willie recognized the sound and he began to tremble anew. "That's a train!" he said aloud to himself.

As if to confirm what he'd said, a whistle shrilled in the night. Clickety-clackety, clickety-clackety, clickety-clackety, the train drew nearer. Willie stepped off the tracks and peered into the darkness. He should have been able to see the train's headlight by now, but there wasn't one.

Clickety-clackety, clickety-clackety, clickety-clackety, clickety-clackety, closer and closer. It just couldn't be. Suddenly, the whistle blared almost on top of him, but there was no train to be seen. The frightened man stood frozen in terror beside the tracks. He turned to look at Bostian's bridge. He could feel the wind of the passing locomotive, but there was nothing there that he could see.

Suddenly there was an awful screeching sound, like brakes battling momentum, followed by a tremendous crash. Willie could hear the roar of rushing steam. Then, the awful sound of agonized moans and screams began.

Willie stood there, frozen in complete horror and shock. He tried to scream, but nothing would come out. And try as he might, he just could not get his legs to move. The noises from the ravine finally stopped after what seemed like forever. Willie stood completely still, breathing heavy and fast. His heart was in his throat, beating fiercely, its thumping filling his head.

After a minute of silence, there was another sound. Willie heard the crunch of footsteps on gravel. He looked up to see a shadowy form approaching him from across the bridge. The terrified man remained frozen, unable to make a sound or to move. As the figure came closer, Willie couldn't make out too many details; it was just too dark. But the man was wearing some sort of dark uniform!

"Why hello, Willie boy!" the figure called as he pulled out a pocket watch. "Do you know what time it is?"

That did it. His shock broken, Willie let out a horrified scream, threw up his hands, turned, and ran away as fast as he could, leaving the inquisitive figure standing there in the dark. He ran all the way home and vowed never again to walk alone on that stretch of track at night. He'd never forget the night he met Linster's spook.

As it turned out later, the figure Willie encountered that night was not the ghost of the unfortunate Linster. It was an Iredell County deputy sheriff who'd been walking along the tracks after his vehicle broke down and who just happened to know Willie. Both would laugh about it years later.

Willie has passed on himself now. One wonders if he ever met the real Linster in the great beyond.

Tom Dooley and his Women

Wilkes County

"Hang down your head, Tom Dooley . . ." These words are from the folk ballad popularized in the late 1950s by the Kingston Trio. A big-screen movie was made too, featuring a young Michael Landon in the title role. The story is based on events that took place just after the Civil War.

Thomas C. Dula was a veteran of the Confederate States Army, having served as regiment musician in the 42nd Regiment, North Carolina Infantry. One month before General Lee surrendered the degraded remnants of the Army of Northern Virginia at Appomattox Courthouse, Tom was captured by Union forces and taken to Point Lookout, Maryland, as a prisoner of war. In June 1865, Tom was released from custody, having taken the oath of allegiance to the Union. He came home to Happy Valley, the area where Wilkes and Caldwell counties meet.

Tom was well known throughout that region as a "ladies' man." He played fiddle for the local square dances and was a popular young man around the community. Tom's special passion, however, was reserved for Ann Melton. She was reputed to be the most beautiful woman in Western North Carolina. She and Tom shared a steamy relationship, even though Ann was married.

Tom also knew a young woman named Laura Foster, Ann's cousin. Over the years, legend has rendered Laura as near sainthood. The Laura Foster of legend was a beautiful, pure creature, led astray by the lascivious Tom. However, Laura probably was neither as innocent nor as beautiful as the legend depicts. John Foster West, an emeritus English professor at Appalachian State University, reported in both his books on the Dula legend that Laura had a reputation for wildness, and that this is how Tom got to know her. In any event, Tom's relationship with Laura would prove fatal to them both.

Tom resumed his liaison with Ann upon returning home and began seeing Laura in March 1866. Somewhere along the way, Tom contracted syphilis. Though evidence suggests that he may have gotten it from a third woman, Ann's first cousin Pauline, Ann blamed Laura (who had probably gotten it from Tom). She threatened to kill Laura. Tom himself had mentioned "putting through" (stabbing) the one who'd infected him.

Early one morning in May 1866, Tom showed up at the home of Wilson Foster, Laura's father. It was before daybreak, but Laura got up and went out to talk with Tom. When she came back inside, the girl was quietly ecstatic. After her father went out to tend his chores, Laura packed a bundle of clothes and set out on the mule to meet Tom Dula.

Following a road along the Yadkin River, Laura stopped to talk with her neighbor Betsy Scott, who was washing clothes in the river. She told Betsy that she was going to meet Tom at the Bates place, and they'd run off to be married. The Bates place, in Wilkes County, was six miles from Laura's home in Caldwell

County. It had once been a blacksmith shop but was now abandoned and overgrown with weeds and bushes.

As Laura rode off, she was excited and happy. She loved Tom and was looking forward to sharing her life with him. After crossing the ridge, Laura vanished. She was never seen alive again. No one knew what had become of her. When asked about Laura, Tom grew agitated and replied that Laura never showed up to meet him. When Wilson came looking for his daughter, he seemed more concerned for his mule than his daughter.

Rumors began to fly almost immediately. The Dula-Foster-Melton triangle was well known, and suspicions arose that Tom, Ann, or both, had done away with Laura Foster. Several searches were organized, but no trace was found of the missing girl.

Tom, for his part, showed little concern for Laura. He did take part in two searches, though only halfheartedly. He seemed more concerned that he was a suspect in the investigation. He hotly denied having anything to do with her disappearance. Eventually, the pressures of rumors and suspicion got to Tom. He left the area, bound for Tennessee. Everyone whispered that this sure made him look guilty of something.

Sheriff William Hicks of Wilkes County sent two of his deputies, Jack Adkins and Ben Ferguson, to track him down. The trail led them to the ranch of Col. James Grayson near Trade, Tennessee, where Tom had been working. Tom had left shortly before the deputies arrived, and Grayson led the two lawmen in pursuit of Dula. They caught him a few miles away at Pandora in the Doe Valley community, nine miles from Mountain City on a road leading to Johnson City, Tennessee. The colonel helped the deputies bring him back to Wilkesboro, where he was placed in jail under suspicion of murder. (An interesting note: This illegal seizure and incarceration, along with new evidence, have led to an effort to have Tom Dula pardoned in recent years.)

In early August, Ann Melton asked her cousin Pauline Foster

to go with her to see Laura's grave. She spoke about digging up the body and reburying it in the garden or cutting it into pieces and disposing of them. They walked for a while, then climbed up what is now called Laura Foster Ridge. Pauline refused to go up to the grave which Ann said was between some trees and laurel bushes.

Near the end of August, after having boasted at the general store about knowing where Laura Foster was buried, Pauline was picked up for questioning. When confronted, she initially denied knowing anything. Under pressure, she told deputy sheriffs Adkins and Ferguson of the day she had spent with her cousin Ann and agreed to take them to the area. Searchers began looking in the woods in the area Pauline led them to. One of the searcher's horses shied away from a certain spot. The body of a woman was found in a mound of soft earth a little over two feet deep, along with a bundle of extra clothing. There was a cut place in the dead woman's dress over her left breast, and further examination found a deep stab wound between the third and fourth ribs.

The find caused a sensation in Wilkes County. There was talk of pulling Tom and Ann, who had been put in jail as a result of Pauline's testimony, from the jail and lynching them. To avoid the scene of an angry mob hanging the prisoners from the famed Tory Oak, authorities moved the prisoners to the Iredell County Jail in Statesville. A change of venue was also granted for court proceedings.

Former North Carolina Civil War Governor Zebulon Vance, for reasons lost to history, agreed to defend Tom Dula. He managed to get Tom's and Ann's trials separated. Tom's trial began in October 1866. He denied guilt, but was convicted on circumstantial evidence and sentenced to death. Governor Vance immediately appealed. In 1867, the North Carolina Supreme Court granted Tom a new trial. After several continuances, the second trial convened in January 1868. Once more, Tom was convicted and sentenced to death. This time, the conviction withstood appeal, and Tom's execution was scheduled for May 1, 1868, in Statesville.

As he awaited his fate, Tom continued to profess his innocence. However, the night before he was to die, he hastily wrote the following confession:

Statement of Thomas C. Dula—I declare that I am the only person that had any hand in the murder of Laura Foster. April 30, 1868

Much debate has ensued over the years concerning this sensational last-minute confession. Some contend that it was a conscience-cleansing effort by a killer before he faced his creator. Others believe it was an effort to save Ann Melton from the same fate—one last act of love from a doomed lover. If this was true, it worked. Ann was later acquitted, largely based on Tom's confession. Either way, we will never know what motivated Tom that last night.

At 2 p.m. the next day, after a two-hour speech in which he once again professed his innocence, Tom Dula was hanged from a crude gallows near the train yards. His sister took the body home to Elkville (now Ferguson) and buried him on their cousin's farm beside the Yadkin River.

Though Tom's note and court proceedings cleared Ann Melton officially, suspicion never left her. For the remainder of her life, people grumbled that Ann had gotten away with murder. Some even wondered if Tom might have been completely innocent after all. Stories began to spread that Ann was a witch.

Many different versions of the story have arisen over the intervening decades. As the result of reviewing over 250 pages of documents including court records, letters and other historical information, researchers found that Tom may in fact have been completely innocent, and that the "last act of love" theory about his note could well be true. As stated previously, a movement is under way to have Tom officially pardoned and a petition has been presented to North Carolina Governor Mike Easley.

Although Pauline's account of being led to Laura's grave by Ann was accepted by the deputies, local residents were never fully convinced that Pauline's story was the truth. Everyone knew about the love triangle and that Pauline had insinuated herself into it. They speculated that Pauline may have had more to do with the murder than she had led authorities to believe.

Strangely, even though it turns out he may have been wrongfully executed, there aren't any ghostly stories about Tom himself. Apparently he rests in peace. Not so for his women. In fact, it may have been the cold hand of vengeance reaching from beyond the grave that took Ann Melton's life.

One night, five years after Tom's death, Ann was riding in a wagon. There was a freak accident, and the wagon overturned on her. People told that Ann had come upon Laura Foster herself, standing in the road. The terrified horses bolted, causing the crash. Ann was speechless in horror at seeing her old nemesis standing before her. Seeing Ann badly wounded, Laura's shade disappeared with a look of satisfaction on its face.

Karen Wheeling Reynolds, a local author who wrote a book and a play on the Dooley legend, first told me of this spectral appearance of Laura. Upon further research, I found a few tidbits from others concerning sightings of the murdered girl. She has been glimpsed along the paths and ridges around Happy Valley, but not in recent memory.

Reynolds also recounted the story of Ann Melton's agonizing death. It is a well-known, terrifying tale. Ann did not recover from her injuries. She lingered for days, extremely ill. The night she passed, she may or may not have made a confession to her husband. We'll never know, because James Melton refused to talk about it.

Ann Melton died in terror and horrible pain. As she succumbed, the horrified woman screamed that she could see black cats climbing the walls. She also declared that she could hear meat frying in hell and smell burning flesh. As she expired, some witnesses swore that black cats did indeed run from under the bed, and that steam billowed from seams in the earth around the house. A few indicated they'd noticed the hellish smells and sounds too. Ann's final breath was a scream of absolute, mind-numbing fear.

Thus Ann Melton, perhaps the last person on earth to know what really happened to Laura Foster, passed into eternity. If all this is true, Ann suffered a far more terrible ending than did Tom Dula.

No one really knows what happened that night in 1866, when Laura Foster vanished, except Laura, her killer (or killers), and God Himself. We will probably never know. But if you should happen to visit Happy Valley and run into Laura Foster's ghost, ask her . . . if you dare. If you see Ann Melton, just run. Her shade couldn't possibly be up to any good!

Benton Hall

The old North Wilkesboro Elementary School building
North Wilkesboro
Wilkes County

I have been researching and collecting "true" ghost stories for years. Sometimes, when looking into the background of one story, details will emerge of another, completely unrelated to the first. This is precisely what happened when I spoke with Karen Wheeling Reynolds about the Dula case. Benton Hall, home to the Wilkes Playmakers, has a resident spook of its own.

Reynolds and several of her colleagues have noticed manifestations of this restless spirit. Things will be moved when no human hand has touched them. There are unexplained noises and footsteps. Several people have heard their names called out, only to find that there was no one else around.

The most common phenomenon, however, is the sudden presence of an overwhelming odor. What it smells like seems to vary depending on who is smelling it. Reynolds and her female colleagues describe it as sweet, like flowers or strong spices. Men, however, detect the odor of decay, much like the smell of rotten potatoes. This would seem to indicate that the ghost likes having the women around, but doesn't care for the presence of men. Is our ghost perhaps the shade of a woman who was hurt in some way by a man when alive? Or could it be a male spirit, jealous of other men being around? Calling to memory similar paranormal phenomena, I would tend to believe the former.

Reynolds explains that the noises and odors have really picked up since renovations began on the old building. "They're especially strong in the basement," she said.

Apparently this is one "haint" that isn't limited to one specific location. One night, the ghost hitched a ride with Reynolds to her home. Seems it was happier at Benton Hall, however, returning with her the next day.

Though disconcerting for sure, there's nothing truly frightening about this particular phantom. It seems playful and amiable, though maybe a little mischievous. One visitor, however, did get quite a fright.

A woman was supposed to come by after hours one night. Though the offices were locked, the main doors were left open for her. The lady came in to take care of her business and heard the sounds of people walking around upstairs. There was also lots of laughing and talking. The woman thought a rehearsal was going on up there. She took care of her own business and decided to go up and say a few words to the players. She climbed the stairs and confronted an empty room. Besides her, the building was completely deserted . . . or was it? The woman left and doesn't go to Benton Hall alone at night anymore.

Who is the ghost who walks the floors of Benton Hall? The building was built in 1913 and served as a school into the 1970s. Thousands of feet have trod those floors. Is it perhaps a teacher, returning to these hallowed halls of learning? A student? Or maybe someone from before the school was built? In any event, the Wilkes Playmakers seem content to live with this guest from beyond. After all, no one seems to have been hurt . . .

"We Just Lost Our Heads"

Near Boonville
Yadkin County

Moonshine. Rot Gut. White Lightnin'. Popskull. All these are aliases for that famous home-cooked brew so popular in the South. Many yet alive remember stories of the heyday of moonshining and Prohibition, grandpa's or great-grandpa's still, and the great lengths they would go to in order to protect them from "revenuers." Some hair-raising tales came from these efforts.

One such story comes to us from rural Yadkin County, near Boonville, East Bend, and Rockford, in the late 1800s. It is a grisly tale, one which terrified my mother, Katie Lineberry Renegar, when she was growing up in the 1930s and 1940s. It was made even more frightening by the fact that the events described supposedly took place within a mile or two of her family home.

A farmer and his three sons were known for making a particularly serious brand of corn mash whiskey. Their recipe and the location of their still in the bottoms of the Yadkin River valley were closely guarded secrets. It was told that they were perfectly willing to do away with anyone who ventured too near.

One evening, three young men were walking in the woods. Two of them were brothers and the other was their cousin. As they walked along, they talked about girls, horses, and finding adventure. They'd all been heard to speak of enlisting in the army, or perhaps running off together out West, searching for fame, fortune, and a new way of life.

Suddenly the boys found themselves in a small clearing. There stood a huge whiskey still. An old shack from slavery days stood nearby, and all around were jars and jugs—some full, some empty. There were also several large barrels filled with top-of-the-line popskull.

"Whoooeeeee, boys!" the older brother cried. "Look-a-there!"

"Um, I don't like this," the cousin said. "Let's get out of here."

"Awww, don't be a sissy!" the younger brother chided. "Come on, let's have us some!"

"Are you crazy?" the cousin demanded. "What if these 'shiners come down here an' catch us?"

Try as he might, the boy just couldn't get his cousins to listen to reason. They opened up one of the gallon jugs and began to drink down the potent liquor. It wasn't long until both brothers were hopelessly drunk. The boys tried to get their cousin to join them, but he steadfastly refused.

It was beginning to get dark, and as the shadows grew longer and longer, the sober young man grew more and more nervous. One brother lit a couple of lanterns and sat down on a stool. The other collapsed on the ground. Both laughed uproariously.

"Come on, you clowns!" the cousin cried, desperation coloring his voice. "Let's go 'fore they come back!"

The cousin suddenly felt cold steel at his temple. Click.

"Too late, boy," a gruff voice said softly from behind him. "Why don't you turn around, real slow-like now, ye heah?"

The two brothers stopped laughing and rose to their feet. Cold fear showed in their eyes, and their mouths were both gaping in shocked horror. Slowly, the cousin raised his hands over his head and turned to face his captor.

An old farmer stepped from the shadows, a double-barreled shotgun held to the cousin's head. The man's three sons emerged from the darkness and grabbed the other two. Frozen in fear, they offered no resistance.

"What 'chall doin' heah?" the older man demanded.

"Nothin', sir!" the cousin responded. "We were just walkin' along and stumbled on this place."

"Stealin' mah 'shine, eh?" the farmer observed.

"Naw, sir, I was aimin' to leave some money for what my cousins took, honest I was!" the terrified boy replied. "Really, mister, we didn't mean no harm! We just lost our heads a bit, that's all!"

"What we gonna do, pappy?" one of the moonshiner's sons asked, stepping forward to hold the cousin. "If'n we let 'em go, they'll tell where the still is."

"No, we won't!" the cousin pleaded. "I swear we won't! They're too drunk to remember, and I ain't gonna say nothin'!"

"Shaddup, boy!" the farmer growled. He thought a moment, then said, "Hold onto 'em for a minute, boys."

The three young men herded their three captives together as their father went over to the old shack. In a few minutes, the old man returned with some shackles and chains, left over from when the shack was used to chain up and punish runaway slaves. He tossed them to his oldest son and said, "Chain 'em up together real good, boys."

The three boys fought back, but it was no use. The moonshiners were just too strong.

"Please?" the cousin begged. "Don't hurt us! We just lost our heads a bit, that's all! We'll make it up, honest!"

The old man turned and picked something up. He looked over his shoulder, meeting the cousin's eyes with his own. He snarled, "So, ye lost yer heads, did'ye now?"

The farmer turned around quickly, swinging something in both hands. The cousin's eyes went wide and he opened his mouth to scream, but didn't have time. The blade of an ax sliced through the cousin's throat like paper, and his head went flying. It landed and rolled a few feet, coming to rest facing them. Dead eyes stared in shock.

Even as the farmer had swung, his youngest son screamed, "Oh my God, pappy! No!"

The two brothers screamed and struggled to try to run away, but their restraints and the weight of their cousin's body prevented them. As they stumbled and fell, the 'shiner's two older sons raised their rifles and fired. The two brothers collapsed in a writhing heap. The old man walked over and dispatched each with a clean blow, severing their heads.

There was blood everywhere. The 'shiner and two of his sons stood surveying their grisly work. The third son was over by the shack, crying and vomiting. One of his brothers went into the shack and came out with some shovels.

The farmer walked over to his son, took him gently by the arm and said, "Get yerself together, boy. It had to be done. Yer brother's right. They'd a told, sure as the world!"

"Why, pappy?" the young man sobbed. "They're gonna hang us for sure when they find them boys!"

"We ain't gonna hang, 'cause they ain't gonna find 'em!" the father told him. "Now, stop yer cryin' an' help us clean up an' bury this mess! Fer yer mama's sake, boy, move!"

Something in his father's voice reached through the heartbreak and delirium to the frightened boy. His face remained ashen, but he stopped crying and pulled himself together. He set about helping clean up.

The four collected all the burlap sacks they could and fetched some blankets from a wagon parked nearby. Each severed head was wrapped in several burlap sacks, and the bodies were bundled up in blankets. Everything was then dragged to the wagon and a horse was brought to hitch to it. They transported the bodies a short distance up the old path. In an open spot, the corpses were buried in a deep, common grave. Dry brush was scattered over it to hide the disturbed earth.

Dawn was breaking as they finished their horrible task. They had chores to do. Before they left the gravesite, the father said sternly to his sons, "We must never speak of this. Ever. It never took place, and we never saw them boys." They left the burial site and went about their business as usual.

It wasn't long before note was taken of the three missing boys. There was some searching done. The farmer and his two older boys volunteered to help, but the youngest was bedridden with a fever. The searches were rudimentary, however, because everyone knew of how they'd always talked about running off together. Even their families didn't think too much of it at first. One must remember that the world was a vastly different place back then. Countless people left old lives behind to start anew elsewhere. Some left loved ones behind and were never seen or heard from again. There was probably a little concern among immediate family members when no letters arrived detailing new adventures, but nothing came of these concerns. Their loved ones never did find out what became of their lost boys.

Eventually, a barn was built over the secret grave, and a house went up a few yards away. A wider road was cleared from the house down to the river. The new barn stretched across the old path, and a gate closed off the path through the barn.

Almost from the moment the home was occupied, strange things began to happen. At night, the clanking of chains could be heard outside, along with loud, awful moans. And, mysteriously, no matter how securely the gate across the path through the barn was locked, it would be standing wide open the next morning. This happened even when it was chained and padlocked. The next morning, the gate would stand open, the broken lock lying on the ground and the chain missing.

A new tenant moved into the house with his family. He'd heard the place was haunted but he was skeptical, though it was obvious something was amiss. There had been a rapid succession of owners and tenants, but none stayed more than a few weeks. The longest stay had been two months; the shortest, one night. The house had stood empty for some time before the new tenant came. The price was exceptional, and this man decided he couldn't let some spook tale keep him from living there. His wife wasn't so sure at first, but her husband's confidence won her over . . . much to both their regrets.

Sure enough, their first night the two were awakened by awful moans coming from the direction of the barn. The clanking of chains rattled their nerves. The husband went to the window and reached to pull the curtain aside. His courage failed, however, when the noises seemed to be getting closer. The ghostly sounds passed by the house and moved down the hollow toward the bottoms. Eventually, they faded away into the distance. The couple didn't sleep the rest of the night.

After some nights of this, the man finally called on his father-in-law and brother-in-law to come sit up with him and see what was happening. They were determined to solve the mystery once and for all. That night, they took up a position in the trees near the front of the barn, each carrying his rifle. As midnight drew near, the three men grew silent and tense as they waited.

At precisely 12 a.m., there arose from the barn the sounds of spooked farm animals. Suddenly, an awful, mournful groan emerged from the night. The hairs on each man's neck and arms stood on end. They readied their weapons.

The clear sound of rattling and clanking chains came to them from the barn. It was faint at first but grew steadily louder. Then a hair-raising chorus of painful moans and mournful sobs filled the night. Each man's knees were knocking, and a tight coldness gripped their hearts.

Suddenly, the lock on the gate exploded and fell to the ground. The heavy gate swung open of its own volition. The trembling men raised their rifles, ready to shoot. But what came out of the barn was nothing they expected and nothing they could kill. For they were already quite dead.

Three men, chained together, emerged from the barn. Their clothes were filthy and moldy. The horrible sounds were coming from bloody stumps where their heads should have been! One by one, the three men watching this horrific scene dropped his rifle, staring in terrified wonder at the spectacle. They huddled together, shaking violently, in complete shock and horror.

The three headless interlopers continued to trudge along the path, bellowing mournful cries into the night, their chains and shackles clanking loudly. The terrified men watched as the corpses marched past the house, turned on the road, and moved down it toward the river bottoms. They continued to watch until the horrible phantoms disappeared in the darkness. The grisly sounds continued to be heard for some time after, eventually fading way into the distance.

That was that, and that was enough. The family moved out the next day and the house was empty again. The manifestations continued into the 1920s and 1930s. Succeeding generations of tenants reported strange incidents and awful noises. And the spooks themselves were seen on a few other occasions, though never quite so dramatically as they were that awful night by those three brave men.

No one could figure out what it meant. Why did these chained wraiths perform their nightly march? Were they the spirits of slaves tortured in the woods before the Civil War? No one alive seemed to know what caused the restless ghosts to rise.

But someone did know. One old man knew why the ghosts walked. After all, they'd been haunting his conscience for several decades. This knowing soul was the last of the old moonshiner's sons, the one who had protested all those years ago his father's butchery of three poor young men.

The old man had never told anyone about what had transpired. His brothers had families, and thereafter, they'd lived fairly exemplary lives. He hadn't wanted to sully their names with something their domineering father had caused. Also, he somewhat feared his strong-willed father's possible reach from beyond the grave. After all, if the murdered boys came back, might not his father come for him if he told?

Now, however, he was an old man. Death already seemed to be stalking him. He resolved to confess the truth before he went to face his judgment. Legend says that he confessed everything to a close family friend on his deathbed. As the families of the murdered boys were long gone, it was decided that their grave should not be disturbed, though it was agreed that someone should say a prayer over them, which was done.

Shortly after the old man died, the headless apparitions ceased their nightly march at last. Years later, lightning struck the barn and it burned to the ground.

There are those older folks who affirm this story, declaring it genuine. Others scoff at it, saying it was just a tale made up to scare people away from the property, in order to keep an old still safe. My mother won't say either way. She will only say that it was a very real and frightening tale to her and others when she was very young, and that she and her siblings would never go near the place at night, for fear the ghosts might choose that moment to reappear.

Dr. Benbow Whips a Ghost

East Bend
Yadkin County

People tend to think of the twentieth century as the era of the automobile, and associate travel by horse or wagon to be something from the more distant past, such as the Civil War or the Old West.

The truth is, in the rural south especially, people continued to move about by horse and wagon, or even on foot, well into the 1930s and beyond. My Uncle William and my dad, Flay Renegar, insist that this is why people used to see spooky things more often and tell more ghostly tales back then than they do now. On foot, in a wagon, or on a horse, the pace is more leisurely and you are more exposed to the open. In a car, you are moving a lot faster, and you are more enclosed and isolated from what is going on around you. Unless it is one of those infamous "vanishing hitchhikers," you could now drive by within a few yards of something, either spectral or natural, and never see it.

In the old days, country doctors still made house calls, often traveling in their sturdy Huff buggies, pulled by their faithful horses. These dedicated physicians ranged far and wide at all hours to tend the sick.

One such dedicated man was Dr. Thomas "Tom" Benbow. He grew up in East Bend, the son of a well-known and respected physician, Dr. Evan Benbow. The Benbow house still stands on East Main Street, beside the historic Davis Brothers' Store, and across from the old Yadkin Valley Hotel and the T. D. Smitherman General Store.

Dr. Benbow's duties took him all over eastern Yadkin County and across the river into Forsyth County. A broken bone here, a high fever there, a baby to be born—Dr. Benbow did it all.

It was a dark night. The only light came from a thin crescent moon and the running light of Dr. Benbow's buggy. He had been out to tend to a patient in the Flint Hill community. It was very late, and he was tired and ready for bed. Luckily, it wouldn't take too long to get home. The horse and buggy were moving along at a pretty good pace as they moved north along the Flint Hill Road. Dr. Benbow relaxed a little. He knew that the horse could find his own way home if need be.

Suddenly, less than half a mile south of Baltimore Road, the horse began to act very nervous. Dr. Benbow snapped alert, looking around. "What's the matter, boy?" he asked. "What's got you so spooked?"

A sudden, sharp noise below and to his right just about stopped the poor man's heart and caused him to nearly jump through the ceiling of his buggy. The startled doctor looked down to see what it was and let out a breath. He began to laugh at himself. It was just a little dog.

"Pooch, you nearly scared the life right out of me!" Dr. Benbow declared. "Run along, now!"

The animal looked up at him. It panted and wagged its tail. It began to bark again and continued to run along beside the wagon, spooking the horse even further. Dr. Benbow started to fear that he would bolt into an uncontrolled flight and crash. "Damn it, dog!" he hollered. "I said git!"

All of a sudden, the horse stopped. He whinnied wildly, snorted, and reared up on his hind legs. "Whoa!" Dr. Benbow cried in alarm as he picked up the reins. "Whoa, I say!" The doctor peered into the dark to see what had caused this new problem. By the dim light of the moon and that cast by his running lantern, he could see a figure stepping from the bushes. Though he couldn't make out features in the dark, Dr. Benbow thought it was one of the farmers he knew who lived out here, so he wasn't really frightened. He did put his hand on the whip beside him though, just in case. "Mister, is that your dog?"

The shadowy figure was silent. Had he nodded? The doctor thought so. "A yappy little mutt, ain't he?"

The man stood in silence. The dog looked from the shadowy form to Dr. Benbow and back. He wagged his tail and began to bark again. The doctor was angry now. He really wanted to get home. "Mister, how about making your dog shut up and go on?" he demanded. "He's spooked my horse something awful!"

The man continued to stand there in stubborn silence. The dog was barking ceaselessly. Dr. Benbow was furious. What kind of joke did this idiot think he was playing? It was too late for this kind of shenanigans. The doctor picked up the whip and shook it. "See here!" he growled. "Shut that animal up now or I'll whip him good for you!"

The man stood quiet. The dog barked. Dr. Benbow had had enough. He lashed out with the whip. He was amazed and shocked to see it pass right through the barking animal. He blinked. He must be seeing things. The doctor swung again and again. Each time, the whip passed through the still-barking dog's back. It wagged its tail.

"Uh-oh," the doctor's mind thought. "This is not good." But Dr. Benbow was not an easily frightened man. He looked up at the silent, shadowy form regarding him. He cracked the instrument sharply at the brazen man. It passed right through him too.

Cold fear gripped the doctor's heart. His pulse pounded in his head, and a cold sweat broke out on his forehead. But Tom Benbow was a doctor. With the utter calmness of manner only a seasoned physician can muster in a crisis (or was it merely utter shock?), he looked at the figure's dark visage and said, "Oh, so you're a spook, are you? Well . . . you know what? I don't believe in spooks!"

The man stood silently. The dog continued to yap. Dr. Benbow averted his eyes to stare directly ahead, at the hindquarters of his horse. "Come on, boy, giddy-up!" he called out in the most level voice he could summon, "Let's get on home and leave this aggravation to his business!"

The horse seemed to take courage from his master's calm. He snorted at the quiet man a couple of times, then slowly began to pull the buggy past the dark figure, who turned on his heel and walked back into the bushes.

The dog stayed beside the buggy, barking his head off as he went. However, his confidence now restored, the big animal largely ignored the little beast. And as Baltimore Road came into view, the ghostly mutt and his annoying bark simply faded away. Dr. Benbow arrived home without further incident.

The next day, he went back to look around. Not surprisingly, he found no trace of the nocturnal interlopers. Later on, Dr. Benbow would tell of this remarkable encounter over and over, more in amusement than anything else.

Dr. Benbow has been gone for years, now, and, sadly, so is that archetype called the country doctor. But their legacy lives on, in stories, and in the medical professionals of today. I'll bet you wouldn't find one of them out whipping some spook, though.

John Goolsby

Near N.C. 67
Forsyth County

My uncle, William Spillman, who is married to my mother's sister, Mary Ruth, told me quite a few of the stories in this collection. He was born in 1931 in East Bend, and many of the tales were already well established legends when he heard them as a boy.

One of the most familiar tales of his youth concerns an old two-story house near Donahah, just across the Yadkin River in Forsyth County. The house still stands on the left side of Payne Road just after you turn onto it from Donahah Road. (This Payne Road is not to be confused with the infamous road of the same name in Stokes County, which is reputed to be haunted and is featured in Burt Calloway and Jennifer FitzSimmons' book, Triad Hauntings.) An old store building stands at the corner where these roads meet, a short distance beyond the railroad crossing from N.C. 67.

A certain John Goolsby owned the place in the late 1800s or early 1900s. Little is remembered about Goolsby now, except that he occasionally wore a top hat and a dark cloak. One day, Goolsby walked into a room in his house, sat down, placed a shotgun under his chin, and blew his own head off. Blood and cranial matter were said to have splattered all over the ceiling and the walls.

John Goolsby was buried, and his house went on the market. Several people moved in but few remained for long. You see, Goolsby's spirit refused to leave with his poor body. Strange footsteps echoed through the rooms of the house. Doors would open and close on their own, and things would move around when no one was watching. John was even seen on occasion.

One evening at dusk, a young woman was walking down the dirt road. She observed the Goolsby house, and the untrimmed hedges, as tall as an adult, growing up in front of it. As she neared the walkway to the front door of the old home, a tall figure dressed in black came around the corner of one of the hedges and walked towards her. A cloak billowed from his shoulders, and a top hat rested upon his solemn brow. Not recognizing him, the girl spoke to him nonetheless, "Good evening, sir. How are you?"

The man said nothing. He didn't even look at her as he turned up the pathway and walked to the house. When the girl looked to see if he went into the house, which she knew to be deserted, the figure had vanished. She continued to the store, where she asked if anyone had moved into the old house.

When queried as to why she'd asked, the girl described her encounter with the stranger.

When the people present began to laugh nervously, she demanded, "Why are you laughing? That man was rude to me!"

The store's owner guffawed, "He wasn't rude, honey, because he wasn't real! You just described ol' John Goolsby who died many years ago. He shot himself in that house!"

The girl collapsed heavily in a nearby chair. She refused to walk back by the house, waiting until one of the men volunteered to give her a ride home in his wagon. She would never venture by the place again by herself after dusk.

The rumors and legends about the Goolsby house were already decades old when William's sister, Mattie Lee, and her husband Floyd moved in shortly after World War II. From the start, they heard strange noises and noticed that things would be moved out of place.

My uncle himself would have one weird experience in the Goolsby house when he was sixteen. Occasionally he would ride with a local mailman, Charles Burchett, in his wagon to go pick up mail from the train at Donahah. Sometimes, William would walk over to his sister's and spend the night.

It was one such night when he experienced one of Goolsby's activities. Everyone was upstairs, getting ready for bed. Suddenly, a horrendous crash sounded from below. It sounded as if Mattie's heavy china cabinet had overturned and shattered every dish and glass in it!

"What the hell?" Floyd gasped. "William, go on down there and see what's going on!"

My uncle bravely went down the steps to check things out. He looked all around, but could find nothing amiss, certainly nothing to have raised such a ruckus. All the doors were locked, and nothing was out of place. The china cabinet stood undisturbed, all its contents intact. William went back upstairs but left early the next morning.

Mattie Lee had a baby and Floyd wanted her to take it easy. He decided to hire someone to come stay with them and help take care of chores. Thus Beulah came to the Goolsby house.

One evening after supper, Beulah was in the kitchen washing dishes while everyone else gathered in the living room. As she scoured, she noticed a man that came through the doorway from the back porch. He was dressed in black and wore a black hat. He walked past, behind her. Thinking him a neighbor or perhaps the parson, Beulah spoke to him without looking directly at him. The man didn't say anything, but continued on into the living room. The housekeeper thought nothing of it and continued with her chores.

A few minutes later, when she'd finished the dishes and dried off, Beulah walked into the living room where everyone was talking and laughing. Floyd and a couple of guests were talking about President Truman, and Mattie was rocking the baby. The stranger was nowhere to be seen.

A look of confusion crossed Beulah's face. "Why, Beulah, what's the matter?" Mattie asked, looking up from the baby.

"Where'd he go?" Beulah asked.

"Who?" asked Mattie.

"That man," the housekeeper replied.

"What man?" Floyd turned to her.

"The one that just came in from out back," Beulah answered. "He came in the back door and walked right on in here."

"Nobody's come in here but you, Beulah," Floyd told her, eyeing his wife anxiously. "Not since we all did."

"Besides, no one could've gotten in that way," Mattie spoke up. "I locked both screen doors myself an hour or so ago!"

Confused, Beulah turned and went into the kitchen. Floyd and one of the others followed. They went out onto the back porch. The porch was walled in, with a screen door at each end, and on one side was an old wall. Sure enough, both doors were locked. That was too much for Beulah. She left immediately.

Shortly thereafter, Floyd, Mattie Lee, and the baby moved out as well. "There's just too much going on in that house," was their reply when asked about it. "John Goolsby can have his house, and welcome to it!"

It has been many years now since those days when my uncle and his sister's family had to deal with John Goolsby's restless phantom. Over the years, the stories have faded, and Goolsby has receded into the mists of time. Does he still roam the rooms of his former earthly abode, or does he finally rest in peace? The house is occupied now, so it probably wouldn't be prudent to go traipsing around there. John doesn't seem interested in communicating with strangers anyway.

The Red Room

Near Mocksville and Cooleemee
Davie County

No, this isn't Jack Nicholson wielding an ax in the movie adaptation of Stephen King's "The Shining." Nor does it involve some grand hotel set high in the Rocky Mountains. It does concern an old dilapidated two-story house in rural Davie County, North Carolina, a small county in the Piedmont.

The home in question sits at the end of a dirt road. The road runs beside an old church, which is reputed to be haunted as well. No one has lived there in years, and weather, time, and neglect continue to take their toll. The decaying house has built quite a reputation over the years. Local teens and young people from surrounding areas have heard stories about the place, and many have visited, hoping to see evidence of supernatural activity. These "ghost busters" have come in search of the Red Room.

Supposedly, if you drive down to the house at night, once your headlights cross the windows of a front corner room, you can see an interesting, spooky sight. The walls, painted white, will allegedly begin to change color. The longer you let your lights shine in the room, the more they change. Eventually, they turn to a bright scarlet, much like blood!

The story is that a happy family once lived there. The family of four seemed the perfect image of rural life. But under this serene surface ran a strong undercurrent of something dark . . . evil. No one suspected anything was wrong. Therefore, everyone was shocked by the ensuing events.

One dark, rainy night, the father gathered his wife and children in the front corner room. There, in an orgy of blood, he slaughtered them all. His grisly work was frenzied and gory. Blood sprayed all over the walls and ceiling and ran in rivers across the floor. His rage satisfied, the killer stepped out of the house into the rainy night. He turned back to look at his home. As he regarded the edifice, an awful chuckle arose from his lips, growing into a wild, maniacal laugh. The glow cast by the lights inside the murder room shone forth in a sickly, bloody red!

The fate of our villain is shrouded in the mists of time and legend. Some say he was arrested, convicted, and executed for the crime. Others say he went to prison for life, or was confined in a mental institution. Still others say he was never caught and that he started a new life far away. And there are some who say nothing like this ever happened, that the story was made up to scare people away from the neglected property.

A young man named Jeff and some of his friends have no reason to doubt the authenticity of the story. One summer night, they had their own encounter with the red room. The group of young people had heard tales about the old place. The legend of the gruesome murders and the room that glowed red with blood intrigued the boys, so they decided to check it out. As they drove down U.S. 601 towards Mocksville, the boys recounted the different versions of this story and exchanged tales of other local haunted houses. In town, 601 runs into U.S. 64.

They continued on this route until they turned off 64 outside the city limits.

It was darker than any of them could remember. The moon was hidden by thick clouds. It looked like it might rain. They approached the dirt road. An ancient, dilapidated church sat on the corner. As they turned down by it, one boy whispered, "Geesh! That place looks mighty creepy itself! Reckon it's haunted?"

They were all quiet as they rode down the lonely dirt road. Suddenly, the moon burst forth from behind the clouds, offering plenty of illumination. The shadowy edifice of the house loomed before them around the last curve.

The house was dark. The blackness in the windows was thick and foreboding. The headlights shone through the curtainless windows of the murder room, reflecting off the whitewashed walls.

"Keep your lights on those windows!" one boy told the driver as he stopped the car. "They say it doesn't take long!"

The five young men sat in silence. Each held his breath, waiting . . . waiting . . . waiting. They weren't disappointed. Shortly, their eyes widened and their mouths dropped open in great gaping O's.

The walls had begun to take on a reddish hue. At first, it was a washed-out, pale tinge, but as they watched, it grew brighter and darker. After a few moments, it was a hard, scarlet red, seeming to have a light of its own. Jeff shivered. It reminded him of blood.

"Let's go in and check it out!" one of the boys cried, opening his door.

"Are you crazy?" demanded Jeff. "Don't you see the same thing I do?"

"Yeah, but there's probably a perfectly logical explanation for it!" the other boy replied. "Like a red carpet, or something. I've just got to know!"

"Come on, Jeff!" another friend chided him. "Surely you don't believe in all that ghost crap, do you?"

"I just don't know," Jeff replied honestly.

The decision was taken from his hands. The driver shut off the car, turned off the lights, and got out, putting his keys in his pocket. The others followed. Unwilling to be left in the car alone, Jeff got out too.

They approached the front door, turning their flashlights on. One of them tried the doorknob.

With a loud, resounding creak, the door swung open. The boys entered one by one. Jeff and the others looked around, playing the beams of their lights along the walls and ceilings. A thick layer of dust covered everything, and giant webs hung all over the place. What furnishings were there rested under dust-covered sheets.

"Man, this is creepy!" one boy whispered.

"Yeah," another said softly. "Just like in the movies!"

"Boo!" the driver yelled, echoing throughout the house. Jolted, the others jumped and yelped in surprise. They trained their lights upon him and turned to glare at him. He laughed, but the other boys were not amused. "Do that again," one of them growled, "and this place'll be haunted for sure, because you'll be a ghost!"

The group explored the first floor, staying together. They regarded the stairs, but decided not to go upstairs. The staircase did not look very stable, and none of them wanted to risk a broken leg to find out.

At last, they stood before the open doorway of the room where the murders supposedly occurred. Here, they paused. No one wanted to be the first to go in. "Oh, for crying out loud!" Jeff sighed, elbowing his way to the front and going in. The others followed.

They shined their lights all around. The walls were painted

white. There were hardwood floors in all the rooms. The hypothesis that perhaps there was a red carpet was dispelled. There was absolutely nothing in the room that could cause the red glow.

"Look!" Jeff cried, pointing to where three of the flashlight beams shown on one wall. They all did.

The wall was changing, both in color and texture. It was turning red and looked more and more like blood. They could even smell the coppery odor of the life-sustaining liquid. Not only this, but the wall appeared to be getting wet, slick, and sticky.

"Auuuuuugh!" one boy screamed and ran. They heard him tear out of the house and head for the car.

"Let's get out of here!" the driver yelled. They all bolted.

As Jeff ran, the hair on the back of his neck stood on end. As he rushed for the door, he sensed they weren't alone in the house. Someone, or some thing was watching them. He could feel eyes boring into his back. He didn't turn to see what or who it was—he knew he'd see something that would scar him for life, if it didn't drive him completely mad.

The boys scrambled out of the house and raced for the car. Even as the last one jumped in, the driver cranked the vehicle, slammed the transmission into reverse, and spun it around. He shoved it into gear and slammed his foot down on the gas. Dirt and gravel spat from beneath the tires as the car spun away from the looming edifice. Clouds once more covered the moon, plunging them into total darkness, save the headlights and the glow of the dashboard. They were all breathless with fatigue and fear.

Just before they rounded a curve, Jeff looked back. A light shown into the darkness from the windows of the murder room. The Red Room. Silhouetted in the dim, sickly, red glow at one window was a shadow. Someone was watching their escape!

Jeff turned to stare straight ahead. He did not say a single word. They didn't even slow down at the end of the dirt road. Tires wailed as the car spun onto the pavement. In total silence, they made their journey home, each now firmly believing in the reality of the legend of the Red Room. Are ghosts real? Those boys sure think so.

The house remains today, falling further and further into disrepair. Perhaps one day someone will fix it up. Or maybe it will eventually surrender to the elements, as countless other such homes have. No matter what happens, the story of the Red Room will continue to rouse curiosity for another few generations.

The Mitchell River Monster

Zephyr Mountain Park
Surry County

Dark, sinister clouds roll across the sky. Suddenly the full moon bursts forth, shining down on hill and hollow. A huge form, darker than the shadows around it, stirs. Glowing red eyes open and blink several times. Then the savage beast turns its face to the heavens, baring razor-sharp fangs. It throws back its head and lets go a bloodcurdling, canine howl!

Sounds like a scene from one of Universal Studios' old 1930s or 1940s horror movies, doesn't it? Or, perhaps, from one of the later Hammer remakes or the gory Howling series of latter-day werewolf films. Well, it's not—this monster is the real deal.

The Mitchell River meanders through western Surry County. It flows over the dam at Kapp's Mill in Devotion, through the Zephyr Mountain Park area, passes under Interstate 77 and N.C. 268 before emptying into the greater Yadkin River between Elkin and Dobson.

There are several scenic spots along this stream, allowing for fishing, swimming, and hiking. An air of peace is instilled by the sounds of the water lazily moving along. Something dark and sinister lurks behind this peaceful facade, however: the Mitchell River Monster.

For several decades now, people in the vicinity of the river have reported seeing the strange creature. It seems especially fond of the area along Poplar Springs Road, which runs from U.S. 21 in Elkin into Dobson. It's been seen all over the Zephyr Mountain Park region, on dark, lonely nights. It has been seen in open fields, in the woods, along the banks of the Mitchell, and in the road itself.

The creature is big, like a bear, but it is no bear. This beast crouches on all fours like most any animal. But when it moves, the monster rises up on two feet and bounds away, bearing itself more like a man than an animal. It is nearly seven feet tall. It is big and muscular but lithe, and is covered in thick, shaggy fur. Vicious, razor-sharp claws sprout from the tips of fingers and toes. The most distinctive feature, however, is the monster's head. It is huge and canine, with a long snout. Rows of sharp teeth fill the mouth, sharp ears rise over the cranium, and fierce, glowing red eyes shine forth from its terrifying visage. These wolven features distinguish our monster from any bear or comparable animal.

The creature has made dozens of appearances over the years, the first nearly forty years ago. Two men were out running their dogs, coon hunting. It was a clear night, and there was a full moon. The two men picked up their pace as the baying of the hounds changed, indicating they'd treed something.

They approached a stand of trees near the Mitchell River. The sounds of the water flowing by could be heard just a few yards beyond. They pointed their lights up into the tree the dogs had surrounded. Sure enough, a terrified raccoon peered back at them from a high branch.

"This one's mine!" the first hunter said to his partner, raising his .30-06 rifle to take aim.

Suddenly, the dogs began to look around in confusion and whimper. The bravest of the pack turned toward the hill behind the men and began to growl.

"What the heck is eating those guys?" the second hunter called. A shadow passed over them, and he turned to look up at the top of the hill. The second hunter's eyes widened and his mouth dropped open. He backed up and sat down hard, tripping over a root. "Jesus!" he cried. "Oh, sweet Jesus Christ!"

The first man looked over at his companion. The man's face was ashen and a mask of terror. Slowly, he turned to look up at what had the other man paralyzed in fear. A nightmare from his childhood peered back at him from the hilltop. A figure was silhouetted in the full moon. It was huge, close to seven feet tall. It stood in a freakishly human-like manner, front paws resting on its hips. Evil, hungry red eyes glowed in the wolf-like head. It let out a guttural snarl.

Galvanized by primal fear, the hunter turned the barrel of his gun on the fiend and fired. The range was less than fifteen yards, and he saw the impact as the bullet struck the creature full in the chest. The creature seemed more annoyed than hurt, barely flinching. The red eyes narrowed, and the animal, or whatever it was, growled dangerously.

The horrified hunter fired again. His friend took shaky aim and fired too. Five, six, seven times they saw bullets strike the beast. Finally, the seventh bullet hit its left temple. The creature threw back its head and issued an awful, painful howl. It turned and loped off down the opposite side of the hill.

The hunters wisely decided not to give chase. After all, the thing had taken seven shots from a .30-06 and a .30-30 and it barely fazed him. The two men collected their dogs as quickly as they could and left. They agreed not to talk about what they'd seen. No one would believe them anyway.

The next full moon, the monster made another startling

appearance. An Elkin couple was returning home from Dobson. As they neared the Mitchell River bridge on Poplar Springs Road, something crouched in the road ahead of them.

"Is that a bear, George?" the wife asked, excited.

"I don't think so!" her husband replied. "I don't know what the heck it is!"

Suddenly, the thing reared up on two feet! The man slammed on his brakes. The beast took off running, just like a man. The couple watched it until it disappeared into the woods. They went immediately to the police station in Elkin and reported what they'd seen. Surry sheriff's deputies sent to investigate found no animal, but did find broken limbs where it had crashed through the tree line. They reported it must be a bear. The couple swore it was something else.

Thus was born the legend of the Mitchell River Monster. Some scoffed at the tales, saying it just had to be a bear. Others thought it was Bigfoot. A few more superstitious souls whispered that it was something supernatural—a werewolf.

Over the next few decades, the monster would put in countless appearances. One family swore they saw it lurking in the shadows of the tree line along the bank of the river as they swam in broad daylight. Mostly, however, he was seen at night.

One man who lives in the area used to like to mow his lawn at night by the headlights of his riding mower. One night, he had to go inside for a moment. He left the engine running as he got off and went in. He heard an awful noise and rushed back outside. The mower was still sitting where he'd left it, the motor running, but the hood had been ripped clean off and lay several yards away. It was mangled and claw marks were clearly visible. Something made him look towards the woods behind the house, where he saw a shadowy form disappearing into the trees. It was the monster. The man doesn't mow at night anymore.

A few years later, John and his girlfriend were returning to

Elkin from Mt. Airy, via Dobson. It was a moonlit night and very late. As they drove along down Poplar Springs Road, the girl suddenly cried, "What's that?"

John's eyes followed her pointing finger. In a field, something large was moving on all fours. At first, John thought it was a bear, or perhaps a large deer. But when his headlights swept across it, the creature jumped up on its hind feet and took off. Stunned, the two teens watched as it bounded away in great strides. John said later that it ran like a track star, figuring it was moving between forty-five and fifty miles per hour. The creature crossed the field and ran up a hill. It paused at the trees and turned to look at them. Both swore they saw angry red eyes glowing in the dark. Then it turned and was gone. The teenagers continued home in silence.

What is the Mitchell River Monster? Some mutated bear? An undiscovered species? Or is it something not of this world— something supernatural? No one seems to know, except, of course, the monster himself. And so far, he hasn't been sociable enough to stick around and talk. But he's still out there, lurking in the shadows. If you happen to be driving through that area at night and see red eyes peering at you out of the darkness, just keep right on driving. Some things are better left alone.

The Story of the Lawsons

Near Walnut Cove and Germanton
Stokes County

It was Christmas Day, 1929. A heavy snow covered the ground. A large bonfire provided warmth for the crowd of people milling about. In a rocking chair set close by the fire sat a trembling young man, covered in quilts and blankets. A profound sadness filled the young man's countenance, and tears streamed down his cheeks. If only he hadn't left. He could have prevented this! A few yards away, some of the bystanders regarded the boy solemnly. They were sure that, had he been home, the sad young man would have been dead too, along with all his brothers and sisters, and his beloved mother.

They turned to look nervously at the house nearby. Stokes County Sheriff John Taylor stood on the porch, grimly speaking with the coroner, Dr. Helsabeck. The scene inside the cabin was grisly indeed. In the front room, five bodies had been posed, with their hands across their chests, and pillows under their heads. Two of the victims had been shot, and the remaining three had been bludgeoned to death, their heads caved in by

127

the butt of a rifle. There was blood everywhere. On the mantle, a clock's hands were frozen at 1:25, the first shot inside the house having jarred and disrupted its mechanism.

Two other bodies were found beside a barn on the property. Two little girls, one shot in the head with a .25-20 caliber Winchester rifle; the other, shot in the back with a 12-gauge shotgun. Seven members of the Lawson family, murdered! The father, Charlie, was nowhere to be found. Was he dead too? Only Arthur, the oldest son, remained.

Dead were Fannie Lawson, age thirty-seven, her daughters Marie, age seventeen, Carrie, age twelve, Mae Bell, age seven, and Mary Lou, age four and a half months, and two of Fannie's sons, James, age four and Raymond, age two. The Christmas murder of the Lawson family would send shock waves around the world, making headlines in papers as far away as Japan.

Who could have done this awful deed? Was it Charlie? Where was he? Or was it some stranger who had killed the family and done away with Charlie elsewhere? These questions filled the minds of all those standing about the yard. Several armed men had been dispersed across the farm, looking for Charlie's body or for the killer.

Suddenly, a shot rang out in the darkening evening. Everyone jumped at the sharp sound. Arthur moaned and sank down further in the rocker. It sounded like a shotgun and came from the nearby woods. The group of bystanders looked nervously at one another.

Finally, S. C. Hampton, a neighbor of the Lawsons', started off in the direction of the shot. Others followed after him. The man walked down a trail, noticing a lone set of footprints in the snow leading in the same direction.

The evening stillness was now broken by the mournful howling of two dogs. The man knew Charlie had two dogs, Sam and Queen. He moved in the direction of their sad cries. Finally, he came upon them in a thicket. There lay Charlie's two dogs, whimpering softly. Between them was the bloody body of their master. Charlie Lawson had used a stick to pull the trigger of his shotgun, blowing a massive hole in his chest. In his pocket were found two pieces of paper on which were scrawled two cryptic lines: "Troubles can cause . . ." and "No one to blame but . . ." It seemed obvious that Charlie was responsible for everything and that he'd tried, but failed, to write a suicide note. But why had he done it? What possible reason could he have for mercilessly butchering his wife and children?

The family was buried in a huge grave at Browder Cemetery. Arthur never really recovered from the tragedy. He was himself killed in a truck wreck in May 1945. He would not talk about the brutal murders and always blamed himself for the deaths. He was the only one able to stand up to his father, and he believed that, had he not left home to go into Germanton that day, he could have stopped Charlie.

Stories began almost immediately that the Lawson house was haunted. How could it not be? People who passed by at night claimed to hear voices arguing in the cabin. One claimed to have heard gunshots on the first anniversary of the killings. Another arrived home one day, his face ashen. When asked what had frightened him, the man replied that he had seen Charlie Lawson's face peering at him from an upstairs window. This was five years after the murderer ended it all.

For years after the murders, there were tours of the Lawson cabin and property. The blood remained on the floors, fading only with time. There is a story that a note was left on the door from legendary gangster John Dillinger. The outlaw had apparently toured the house earlier in the day though no one had recognized him. Eventually, interest waned and the awful circus ended.

Did Arthur know why his father had carried out such a

ruthless, cold-blooded act? We'll never know for sure. Rumors flew, but the mystery remained. For six decades, a dark family secret was kept by relatives and friends. Finally in 1989, sensing her time was coming to an end and fearing the truth might die with her, a Lawson relative revealed the truth: Marie Lawson had been pregnant and Charlie was the baby's father. Charlie couldn't live with himself and the scandal which was sure to follow. Perversely, he needed to take his family with him and so he slaughtered them.

The mystery was solved—Bruce Jones and Trudy Smith wrote about it in their book, White Christmas, Bloody Christmas. Jones and Smith debunked the ghost stories in their book, saying only that people had trouble sleeping in the murder house. They also described a prank two men played on some unsuspecting teenagers which probably led to further rumors of a haunting. Despite their assurance that the Lawson place was not haunted, stories remained.

Just a few days before the cabin was to be torn down in the 1980s, three young men from Winston-Salem went up to the Lawson place. They'd heard the house was to be razed, and they wanted to see the site of so brutal a set of murders before it was gone forever.

It was dusk as they pulled up to the old property, and they decided not to get out of their car. As they sat there, they thought they saw movement through a dark window. Suddenly, a face appeared in the window. They all gasped. It was a ghostly pale face, with an expression of hatred, staring down at them. The face disappeared, and the front door swung open. The driver quickly turned his car around, and they spun dirt as they took off. They didn't look back to see if the murderer emerged from the shadowy doorway.

The Lawson cabin is no more—the wood from it was used to build a small covered bridge nearby—but the farm remains. Did

Charlie Lawson continue to roam about his property long after his gory act? Did the restless spirits of his wife or children manifest themselves on occasion? Was the crying heard by a couple in the '50s the sound of baby Mary Lou? Are all the gunshots heard over the years the sounds of hunters, or were some of them the ghostly re-enactment of that long ago Christmas tragedy?

The King's Men
Gaston County

Many are familiar with the story of Gen. Nathanael Greene and his efforts to preserve the Patriot army in the South during our Revolution. He kept retreating from the advancing British Army under Gen. Charles Cornwallis, striking at his pursuer in limited raids, finally committing to a full engagement at Guilford Courthouse. The British claimed the field at the conclusion of battle, but General Cornwallis lost a larger percentage of his troops than did Greene, with reinforcements harder to come by for him. The continued retreat and resistance across the Carolinas into Virginia set the stage for the Revolution's final drama at Yorktown Heights.

An earlier battle, however, had turned the tide in the South: the Battle of Kings Mountain, where Americans had fought Americans. Major Patrick Ferguson, a fierce Scots warrior, had gathered a large force of Loyalists at this site on the Carolina border by September 1780. Col. John Sevier and his Overmountain Men marched across the Blue Ridge Mountains from Tennessee

133

and the North Carolina frontier to join fellow Patriots before Kings Mountain, where the Scottish major was digging in. In a spectacular clash on October 7, 1780, the revolutionary militiamen defeated the British and Loyalist forces. Loyalist resistance in the western Carolinas was forever broken, and General Cornwallis broke camp in Charlottesburg (later renamed Charlotte) to begin his fateful pursuit of General Greene.

This episode in American history brings us an enduring legend of two ghosts on a fruitless mission.

Major Ferguson had grown concerned with the gathering Patriot forces. He began to feel his position might be untenable without assistance from the main British force then quartered at Charlottesburg. He sent messengers to Cornwallis with no response and feared his men had been captured. He decided to send local men who knew the area and would blend in better. Consequently, he dispatched two brothers, James and Douglas Duncan, to go to General Cornwallis for reinforcements.

The couriers set out on the Kings Mountain Road, riding hard. After fording the South Fork of the Catawba River, they stopped at an old inn. The tavern owner had been killed by the British that August in the Battle of Camden, and the two brothers sympathized with his widow, who was running the tavern. In return, the woman gave them an extra measure of whiskey. However, the alcohol eased the brothers' guard and the woman discovered they were on a mission to get British reinforcements. She gave them faulty directions, then went to the attic of the tavern to wait for them to leave. She had just taken out her pistols when the two drunken riders appeared below her, mounted their horses and left. She fired first at the man on the right and with the other pistol at the man on the left. One fell forward a bit but straightened up. The other seemed to jerk in his saddle. Neither man fell and the horses rode off into the night.

Several hours later, an innkeeper named Amos Bissell heard a rough pounding at his door and looked down to see what guests were arriving so late at night. He could not see well outside, but could hear two men arguing outside his door. They were arguing over which way to go, and he could hear them blaming a woman for bad directions. Bissell started down his steep, curving staircase to let them in before they woke any of his guests.

Taking his flintlock pistol as a precaution, he unbolted the inn door and looked out. A map was spread on a tree stump and two men were bending over it, using lantern light to find their way. Bissell began walking toward the men, but a strange feeling made him hang back and listen to their conversation. They folded up their map and led their horses away from the stump. As they moved away, Bissell could clearly see that these men were no longer alive. He was so frightened he could barely make his way back to his inn and latch the door.

The desperate plea for help was never delivered, and the British cause was eventually lost.

The Duncan brothers have apparently not given up their efforts to find the general, even after over two hundred years. Their ghostly forms have been seen thousands of times. Locals have reported seeing the two spectral soldiers come riding up and stop short, preparing to ask for directions. From old-time stagecoach drivers to modern motorists, there have been countless encounters with the Tory couriers. Some claim to have seen two greenish corpses in tattered clothes, kneeling at the roadside over a crude map, especially where roads fork. They seem intent on completing their mission, no matter that both the man who sent them and the general he sent them for are both long dead as well.

The soldiers are most often seen in October, around the time of their murders and the battle. They are usually found somewhere along the back roads from Kings Mountain to Charlotte in Gaston County, most often at one of the numerous forks.

They have been known to make unexpected visits on occasion.

One man, we'll call him Charles, will never forget the night the two cadaverous couriers paid him a visit. Charles and his family moved into a house on Kings Mountain Road when he was a teenager. He'd heard the ghostly legends growing up, but hadn't believed in such things. That all changed one dark night in late September 1980. Charles's parents, little brother, and sister had gone into Charlotte to see their older daughter at UNC-Charlotte. Charles did not expect to see them until the next morning and was watching TV late that night.

Suddenly, there was a heavy knock at the front door. Annoyed, Charles ignored it. Who could be knocking at his door at this hour, anyway? He looked at his watch. It was about 12:30. He stayed in front of the TV, curled up on the sofa.

The knock came again. It was louder; more insistent. Charles expelled a sigh. What if it was important? Reluctantly, he got up and went to the door. He threw it open and started to growl, "What the he—?"

The words died on his lips. His jaw dropped open, and his eyes nearly popped from his head. There stood two men in soiled and tattered clothing. They were solid, but their skin had the greenish hue of rotten corpses. Their hair seemed disheveled under their three-cornered hats.

Charles tried to scream, but he couldn't. The hair stood on end all over his body. The two revenants regarded him with dark, emotionless, lifeless eyes. "In the name of King George the Third!" one of the officers rasped, "Can you tell us where to find General Lord Cornwallis?"

"Aaaaarrrrggggghhh!" was the boy's screaming reply. This seemed to startle the ghostly visitors. They vanished before his very eyes. The boy slammed the door, bolted the lock, and raced up to his room. As he lay trembling in his bed, Charles could hear the heavy knocking on the door again. He pulled his pillow over his ears and held it there until morning. When his family returned in the morning, Charles told them what had happened. No one believed him, of course. They thought his imagination had run afoul.

Charles would see the British couriers again, ten years later. This time, his brother and sister were with him, and they saw the ghostly forms as well. The three were driving home from their old high school's homecoming football game in early October. As they approached the fork in the road near their home, two forms appeared out of the mist. It was two men in Revolution-ary-era clothing, and they looked like swollen, bloated corps-es. One of the soldiers tried to flag them down, waving wildly. Charles stomped the gas and roared by the waving figure. His siblings believed him now, at least.

Lydia of the Underpass: Fact or Fiction?

Jamestown and High Point
Guilford County

She is, perhaps, North Carolina's most famous revenant. Hers is a hauntingly tragic tale. She appears late on rainy, dreary nights at the railroad underpass in Jamestown, which crosses over High Point Road (U.S. 29-70A). Her only goal is to get a ride home to High Point.

Her name is Lydia, and she has been on her heartrending errand since 1923. Back then, the road was several yards to the left as you headed towards High Point. The wreck that took Lydia's life occurred on that stretch, at the old underpass.

Lydia and her escort were on their way home from a dance in Raleigh. It was a rainy, foggy night, and the road was slick. Lydia wanted to get home as quickly as possible. They were running very late, and she was concerned how her mother would react.

As they drove, the young couple was probably happily talking as teenagers of any era do. Maybe they even discussed their plans and were looking forward to their future—a future that was not to be.

Suddenly, at the underpass, another car emerged from the foggy darkness. There was no time for either driver to react. The vehicles collided, head-on. Lydia was killed instantly. A young girl, full of promise, snuffed out in a horrible moment.

A year later, Burke Hardison was taking the same route home from Raleigh. It was around 1 or 2 a.m. as he approached the railroad underpass. A movement caught his eye through the rain. There was a girl standing at the side of the road, trying to flag him down.

Hardison pulled over and rolled down the passenger window. "Can I help you, miss?" he asked her. The girl replied that she was trying to get home to High Point. She was worried that her mother would be upset because of how late it was. The kind man opened the door for the soaked girl, offering her a ride. He noticed her beautiful white gown as she gathered it around her and climbed in.

Hardison thought there was something strange, but he couldn't quite put his finger on it. He tried to engage the young woman in conversation, but her words were faint and detached and he couldn't hear her answers although he did understand her name was Lydia. She finally asked him why he was questioning her so, and requested that he should just get her home.

When they pulled into the driveway at the address she'd given, Lydia seemed to hesitate, as if she could not get out. Hardison got out and stepped around to help her. When he opened the door, the girl was gone, leaving only a wet spot on the seat and a small puddle on the floor.

Confused, the man thought maybe she'd jumped out and ran when he had gotten out of the car. He went to the door and knocked. A woman answered and Hardison asked about Lydia. The woman then told him the sad story of her daughter who'd been killed in a wreck at the Jamestown underpass. She sadly thanked him for trying to bring her home.

Over the years, many writers of ghostlore have written about Lydia and her sad, eternal errand. It is the quintessential "vanishing hitchhiker" story. Others over the intervening decades have claimed to see the ghost, including Frank and Lillian Fay in June 1966.

The sightings even continued after the road was rerouted and a new underpass was built. Apparently, the ghost found her way there when cars no longer passed through the original site.

It was at the new underpass that Tom Beasley and his friend Rick Cook saw something in 1976. I called Mr. Beasley after reading about his encounter in Tanenbaum and McGee's book, and he related the story to me.

About 1 or 2 a.m. they were headed to High Point. It was another dreary, rainy night. As they crested the hill and drove towards the underpass, Tom saw a girl in a white dress standing at the side of the road. "Did you see that girl?" Tom asked.

"What?" Rick chided. "You're crazy!"

Tom turned the car around and drove back towards Greensboro. This time, Rick saw her too. They turned around again and headed back. By now, the girl was sitting down by the roadside. Tom pulled over, and Rick rolled down his window. He leaned out to speak to the girl, but didn't say anything. Tom punched his friend's shoulder, but he remained silent. He did it again, and this time, Rick spoke. "Move the car!" he said in a strange tone.

Unsure he'd heard right, Tom asked, "What?"

"Move the car!" Rick said, more forcefully this time. "Just get us the hell out of here!"

Tom took off, spinning tires. As they moved away, he heard the girl begin to shriek, "Come back! Come back! Come back!"

Tom asked Rick what was going on. His friend replied that something had been very wrong, that the girl had looked as if someone had badly beaten her. They did not go back to see.

Later, the two men wondered if they might have come upon

Lydia. A paranormal investigator later told Tom they'd probably truly seen a ghost. Tom Beasley isn't sure either way, but he did tell me that, if he ever saw her again or had it to do over, she would "by God, get in the car!" even if he had to put her inside.

Did Tom and Rick see a ghost? Or could it have been a prank? Or was it some poor girl who'd been in a fight and just happened to be out, coincidentally, at Lydia's underpass? I tend to believe the latter, and I got the feeling maybe Beasley leans in that direction too, though he is open to the idea of Lydia's ghost.

We have always accepted this story as established fact. We have specific, credible witnesses like Hardison and the Fays. And, of course, Tom Beasley and Rick Cook, who saw a girl that rainy night in 1976. And the name, Lydia, which is not exactly an "out-of-the-hat" name. Her name alone is unique enough to lend credence where we may not have accepted yet another "Mary."

She has been well documented. Nancy Roberts, Burt Calloway and Jennifer FitzSimmons, Linda Tanenbaum and Barry McGee, and Terrance Zepke have all written about Lydia. In fact, I had originally planned not to include Lydia in my writing because the story has been done to death (pun definitely intended), and I already had another vanishing hitchhiker tale from my home county.

But something kept gnawing at me. Lydia, I guess you'd say, wouldn't leave me alone. I was especially intrigued by the alleged existence of actual records of the 1923 automobile accident. I finally gave in to my curiosity and began to dig. I very quickly discovered that the supposed records do not exist. There is no record, not even a note or a field report, of the accident at Jamestown, at High Point, or with the Guilford County Sheriff's Department. I found this out with a handful of calls.

In itself, this proves nothing. Records do get lost on occasion, especially when they are part of a decades-old archive. I tried the Highway Patrol, but they did not come into existence until 1929. Next, I tried the Department of Motor Vehicles, but they only keep records of traffic fatalities back ten years. Continued digging and conversations with police officials on the local level revealed that no one there had ever heard of such a record existing. One person at the sheriff's office in Jamestown flatly declared the story a fairy tale.

Needless to say, I was disappointed, but not ready to accept defeat or make up my mind. I was having doubts though. Is our most famous and beloved ghost story true or not?

Next, I contacted the public library in High Point, hometown of our heroine. A helpful employee told me about a group from the library's North Carolina section that did some extensive research into the Lydia legend. They get loads of requests for information all the time. The employee put me in touch with one of the intrepid researchers.

I spoke with Jackie Headstrom, who, with her colleagues, looked into the tale. They came at the story from a different angle. Since no records exist of the accident, they thought perhaps that there would be records of a death, such as a death certificate. The Register of Deeds in each North Carolina county keeps death certificates and records of deaths in their jurisdictions. If Lydia did indeed exist, and died in Guilford County, that county's office would have the records.

Eureka! Right? I spoke to Jackie Headstrom about their research. They found five women who died in Guilford County in 1923 who were named Lydia, or a derivative thereof. This intrigued me and raised my hopes. I began to get excited again.

Four of those women were quickly accounted for, and none of them died at that underpass in a car crash. Age and circumstances clearly eliminated them from being our Lydia. That leaves just one.

This fifth woman raises yet another mystery. Her death records are missing. The record of one Lydie M. Underwood could not be found. We know she was single, and we know she passed away on January 29, 1923. But without that record, we don't know how or where she died.

Is Miss Underwood our Lydia of the underpass? Unfortunately, without the missing records, we cannot know. The date of her death, January 29, roughly fits in with the legend. How old was she? What did she look like? Did she live in High Point? There isn't an obituary for her in any of the papers in existence at that time, but this is the case with all five women on the list. Apparently, that was fairly normal back then. I checked with one of the oldest funeral homes in Guilford County, but they did not bury Lydie Underwood, and they have no record of her either.

Our calling her Lydia comes from the account offered by Burke Hardison in 1924. He said she was rather soft spoken. Perhaps she said Lydie or Liddie instead of Lydia? It's plausible, and certainly possible.

We may never be able to find the answers to these questions. The missing death record for Lydie M. Underwood is the key to everything. If it can be found, it will reveal the truth. Either the record will show Miss Underwood is Lydia, or it will prove, since she is the only Lydia from the list of 1923 deaths who is unaccounted for, that the ghost story is a myth.

We want to believe. Lydia is such a big part of North Carolina ghostlore that it would be very sad and disappointing to a lot of people to find out that she was never there, that she never existed at all. There are those who will refuse to believe it even should that ultimately be the case.

Unfortunately, I am leaning towards that conclusion. Unless proof can be found, I'll have to accept that Lydia is an urban legend—just another vanishing hitchhiker story. We have no record of the wreck. We have no record of a death. We never hear her last name mentioned. We never hear the name of the street or an address where the ghost asks to be taken. Surely someone, in all those years, would have had the presence of mind to get her last name out of her if they picked her up. And surely someone would remember the address. Are we to believe those who picked her up never told anyone where they'd taken her?

Hardison is long dead himself, as are nearly all persons identified as having actually picked her up and talked to her, so we cannot ask them. Surely they told someone, though. Why has no one ever come forward with a last name or real address? "Protecting the privacy of her loved ones" is no longer a viable excuse. Lydia's parents are long dead, as probably are any siblings or other direct relations she might have had. If someone knows something, I would urge them to step forward and tell the truth.

What about Beasley and Cook, who saw someone there in 1976? Unfortunately, neither of them spoke with the young woman they saw, and they did not pick her up, so she never got the chance to give her name or address. Cook did get a good look at that girl, and she scared the bejesus out of him. But we have no way of knowing if she were a ghost or a living girl in trouble. If she was a living person she should come forward, if for no other reason than the peace of mind of the men involved.

So, there it is. The legend of Lydia of the underpass is neither proven nor refuted. The odds are against proof of Lydia's existence ever being found. It is not likely, after all this time, that Lydie Underwood's records will be found. And even if they are, they will probably show that she is not, in fact, Lydia, thus disproving the ghost story forever. Perhaps it is better this way. The legend can remain intact for those who truly believe, as well as those who wonder. She can continue to haunt our thoughts and dreams and fascinate those who love ghostly tales.

I am interested in speaking with any descendants of Burke

Hardison about his account, and whether or not they can provide any further information.

I would also be interested in speaking with any relatives of Lydie Underwood. Perhaps you can provide some closure to this case. Isn't it odd that her records are missing?

Finally, if there is someone out there who can prove that they are a relative of the mysterious Lydia of the underpass, I definitely want to speak with you. Or, if you live at the address where Lydia asks to come to, or have in the past, please contact me through my publisher.

For anyone interested in looking for themselves, here is the "Lydia" list compiled by the workers at the North Carolina Section of the High Point Public Library. This information is a matter of public record.

1. Lydie or Liddie M. Underwood
Date of Death: 01-29-1923
Marital Status: Single
Location in Register of Deeds: Book 10, Pg. 1699
File Status: Missing

2. Lettie Herbin
Date of Death: 03-10-1923
Marital Status: Single
Location in Register of Deeds: Book 10, Pg. 177
File Status: Accounted For

3. Lydia Jane Norwood
Date of Death: 03-28-1923
Marital Status: Married
Location in Register of Deeds: Book 10, Pg. 245
File Status: Accounted For
4. Lydia L. Horney

Date of Death: 05-07-1923
Marital Status: Single
Location in Register of Deeds: Book 10, Pg. 1473
File Status: Accounted For

5. Lydia Jane McCarthy
Date of Death: 12-31-1923
Marital Status: Unknown
Located in Register of Deeds: Book 10, Pg. 1171
File Status: Accounted For

No obituaries could be located for any of these women.

After completing the body of this story, I had the privilege and honor of speaking with North Carolina's premier collector of ghost stories, Nancy Roberts Brown. She is the author of several books on southern ghostlore. All who have come after her owe her a debt of gratitude. She has always been one of my favorite writers, and I was thrilled to talk to her.

Roberts Brown was one of the earliest to write about Lydia. As it turns out, the driver's name was not Burke Hardison. This was simply a pseudonym she created for him in order to protect his privacy. This is a much-used device to protect those who do not wish to have their identities revealed. I have done it elsewhere in this book.

That explained why I could not find Hardison or his descendants. Should one of them come forward, I promise to protect your privacy just as she did.

Miscellaneous Spooks

Years ago, sometime between the World Wars, my Uncle Albert Reavis walked along the Old Coach Road near the haunted woods of the Cox place. Albert knew the ghost stories about the area, but he wasn't afraid. He didn't believe in spirits. Some kidded Albert and said he didn't mind tasting any kind of "spirits."

As he walked along, Albert felt a presence in the woods next to him. He touched the pistol stuffed into his britches and thought, "just let some varmint jump out there."

Next he felt as if something watched him. He looked into the woods and saw not six paces from him a shadowy figure—one with great, glowing, yellow eyes.

Uncle Albert cursed and pulled the revolver out. When he pointed it at the eyes, they stared back at him, unblinking, unconcerned. Uncle Albert fired six times. He emptied the revolver into the figure at point-blank range.

The yellow eyes still looked at him. They hadn't moved an inch.

Uncle Albert lowered the weapon and mumbled, "Well, how 'bout that." He turned, walked a few steps, then broke into a sprint. He never looked back and didn't stop running until he reached his destination.

The road and hollow just a mile or so west of the Cox place is said to be home to a most fearsome ghost: a headless horseman.

For many years nighttime travelers, whether on foot, horseback, or by wagon, claimed to see a horseman, clad in nineteenth-century military dress, riding along with them. He appeared to watch them, although he didn't have a head.

Several members of the Renegar clan saw the spook. Aunt Nat's mother saw him once from their covered wagon. She could have reached out and touched him, though she said this time the soldier had his head.

Bill Reavis had the scariest and most personal encounter with the ghost. Late one night, Bill drove his wagon and team of mules toward his home. As the rig neared the hollow above the Cox place, the mules started acting jumpy. Suddenly a man walked out of the woods, climbed onto the wagon, and sat beside Bill.

Now Bill was never one to turn down a stranger who needed a ride, but he'd never had a passenger with no head. So Bill sat still, afraid to look directly at his rider again. His hands went clammy on the reins, and he couldn't decide what to do. All Bill knew was that he didn't want to lose his own head.

The mules knew what they wanted. They strained so hard at their restraints that their noses nearly touched the ground. They stumbled and almost fell several times. The mules obviously wanted away from the stranger.

The wagon moved several dozen yards before the headless

man stood, jumped from the wagon, and walked rapidly down the hollow.

Bill stopped the mules. Now that he was safe, he watched the stranger walk until he disappeared into the woods. No, he hadn't been wrong the first time. The man had no head.

The mules calmed down and headed for home. Bill sat numbly.

Who was this mysterious stranger? Was he Union or Confederate? When did he die, and how did he lose his head? Legends talk about a skirmish late in the Civil War, or an Indian attack on a wagon train years before, but any explanation is pure speculation.

When my mother was very little, the family lived on the Primm property. One night, they were expecting a friend of her dad's to come by for a visit. Papa, as we grandchildren always called John Lineberry, waited for him just inside the open door. It had gotten pretty dark, and he was about to give up on his friend when he heard an awful scream in the darkness. He recognized his pal's voice.

John immediately got up and took off out the door without a second thought. He had to get to his buddy. He ran across the yard and raced up the dirt road towards the screaming.

As he went, he could hear pounding footsteps as his friend (we'll call him Lester) approached. Lester was screaming wildly as he ran. John could just make out his form approaching in the darkness. "Lester!" he cried. "What's the matter?"

Wham! Lester piled into John, knocking him to the ground. He didn't even slow down, continuing on to the house. John picked himself up and took off in pursuit.

When he reached his house, John found Lester sitting in a chair. He was trembling and pale as death. John's wife, Viola, was trying to talk to the frantic man. John sat down next to him and tried to help calm him down.

When Lester was finally a little more back to normal, John asked, "What was the matter out there, boy? You were screamin' like a madman!"

Lester looked up at John, and his words stuck with my grandfather forever. "John, you'd have run and screamed too," Lester replied, "if you'd met your sister in the road, knowing she was long dead!"

In 1942, when my mother was seven years old, her parents went out one night, leaving the children under the care of Aunt Molly. The kids played with one another until suddenly they heard a commotion out in the barn. They looked out the window, but the night was too dark to see anything, even though the barn was close to the house. Several puppies in a stall of the barn whined.

Mutt, seventeen, Hoover, thirteen, and Paul, ten, decided as the men of the house they would go check the barn. They grabbed a flashlight and trudged off into the darkness.

Once inside the barn the three boys saw the stall door hanging open. Could it be a thief? A bear? They tiptoed up to the stall, while staying close together.

At the doorway, Mutt shined the light into the stall.

Something turned and glared at them. They couldn't tell what it was, but its huge yellow eyes glowered at them. The eyes were as big as flashlights.

For a wordless moment, the boys gaped at each other. Then they screamed and bolted out of the barn. Paul reached the house first. He opened the door, but Hoover rammed into him. Mutt knocked them both aside as he went through the door. Hoover followed, then Paul, who slammed and locked the door.

Something big slammed into the house.

Then whatever it was went under the house. The kids and Aunt Molly thought it would surely come through the floor. Angry scratching accompanied bumps in the floorboards. The kids huddled together in the living room. The bumping and scratching finally stopped, but no one left the huddle until the parents came home.

The next morning everyone looked for tracks in the yard and barn. There wasn't a single clue as to what the thing had been; the only tracks were the boys'. Shortly after, the puppies mysteriously vanished.

They still don't know what it was, but none of the boys ever forgot the thing with the yellow eyes as big as flashlights.

Tips for the Would-be Ghosthunter

Many people who hear or read ghost stories often feel the urge to go and check things out for themselves. Be warned: a lot of so-called haunted houses are no longer in the best of shape. There could be danger of injury in visiting such sites. Also, in some instances, the entity causing the haunting may show a proclivity to violence. Poltergeist cases and demonic possession incidents in particular are not things for the amateur sleuth to tackle. Cases where the people who experienced the haunting felt threatened or were actually attacked by something also fall into this category. Some examples you might find on video of "bad" stories can be found in such movies as *The Entity* and *The Haunted*. Another good example of what can happen in a threatening situation would be *The Amityville Horror*. Though long ago exposed by the late paranormal researcher Dr. Stephen Kaplan as a complete and fraudulent hoax, it is still a good example of what could happen if you mess around with things better left alone.

Most ghosts, though unsettling, are harmless. Of these, the vanishing hitchhikers are the best example. Most of these revenants are just trying to get somewhere, but sadly they never seem to be able to reach their destination. While startling, mostly by the suddenness of their disappearance, there is no evidence that ghosts like these—Lydia and the dozens of Marys across the country—have ever intentionally caused harm to those who have witnessed them. I don't think I'd be afraid to try to engage one of these poor creatures in conversation.

If you must go on a ghost hunt, there are several things you will need to take along, and things you will need to know. There are two cardinal rules to ghost hunting:

1. Never go to a haunted site alone. Should something happen, such as your falling down, breaking through a floor or steps, or getting injured or ill, you need to have a partner along to help or go for help. If you plan to split up, make sure there are four of you, two for each group. It wouldn't hurt to have a couple more people waiting outside or in the car, just in case. You don't want a circus atmosphere, because that won't be conducive for a paranormal occurrence, but safety must come first. Get people you can trust and who are serious about the experience.

2. Always get permission from the property owner to be there. Some people are surprised to realize that the owners of some haunted spots might not want uninvited visitors roaming about. For some it's a property issue, for others it's a safety issue. Get written permission from the owner and offer them a signed release from liability in case they are worried about a lawsuit if you are injured. Some people think this is too much work, but it's actually much easier than you might think. There are always deeds and other records of who owns a property. Would you rather do the preparatory work or be in jail, arrested for trespassing? If you can get the owner to come along, that's even better.

It also might be a good idea to alert local authorities so they'll know what's going on while you're there, and tell any neighbors right before you go in so they won't call the police or come over and interfere.

Watch for hoaxes. Scout the locale with a friend before you bring in the team. Look for suspicious wires, hidden doors, concealed film projectors and sound systems. If the lights are going to be out, two good ideas are to seal the room with everyone inside who is going to be there, and place masking tape across door frames and windows. Also, you can spread salt or powder of some kind along the walls and in front of doors and windows. If anyone enters the room while the lights are out, you will see where the powder has been smeared if doors or secret entrances are used, and any fake spook will leave footprints behind. Just be sure everyone remains in one place during the investigation. The tape will be broken if anyone perpetrating a hoax should enter the room after you've sealed it. Do not warn the owner until you are in the room. This will prevent him/her from warning any would-be accomplice in a hoax.

There are also some basic supplies and equipment you will need. These are necessities:

• A complete first-aid kit. Better safe than sorry.

• At least one flashlight per person, with fresh batteries.

• Extra batteries for all flashlights.

• A basic tape recorder for each team, with two or three tapes for each recorder. External microphones are better, but not an absolute necessity.

• A 35-mm camera for each team—each individual if possible—with several rolls of film per camera. High speed film (800, 1000, or 1600) is the best. Digital cameras are okay too. The biggest plus with digital is there is no break in the chain of custody. With most models, you can view the image immediately. You don't have to give it to a lab to develop (which risks contaminating the image) but can take it straight to your computer if you catch something interesting. In fact, some ghost hunters swear they are actually more apt to catch such things as orbs or faint apparitions. However, they are also more prone to catch a dust particle, which will produce an orb-like effect. I prefer 35-mm, though I have caught some interesting things on digital.

• Blankets and coats are essentials, especially during the winter months. Be sure to dress appropriately.

• Bring ample amounts of prepared foods and snacks, two or three bottles of water per person, and any medications needed by team members, such as prescriptions for chronic conditions, current illness, allergies, and Tylenol or other pain relief.

• Each individual should have a small notepad and two or three pens or pencils, to record their impressions of the scene and any activity they witness. Different perspectives can be helpful in recording an actual apparition, or in catching a hoax.

• Bring at least one set of walkie-talkies for each team. Keep them turned down low, and use them only when necessary. Always speak in soft tones until it's time to go.

• Bring matches or a lighter in case the flashlights fail, and to thaw frozen car locks in winter.

• At least two fully-charged cell phones are also a necessity, in case outside help is needed.

There is some optional equipment you might want to consider as well. A video camera with a couple of extra tapes per team can be helpful, especially in detecting hoaxes. Infrared film has been known to register a spectral presence in still photography where regular film has not always been able to catch a spook.

According to some paranormal investigators, ghosts can

cause strong electromagnetic fields or discharges. Therefore, you might consider obtaining an EMF detector. They can be found at most electronics stores. Thermometers can also be useful in determining changes in temperature and cold spots. They can also help in detecting hot spots. Though much more rare than cold spots in hauntings, they do occur.

A good, old-fashioned compass can be useful too. The pointer of a magnetic compass sometimes spins like a dervish in the presence of paranormal activity, but be careful of relying on them completely. A nearby TV, radio, or other electrical device will contaminate your reading.

Before embarking on the actual hunt/investigation, do some research into the past of the site. Check newspaper records, court or police records, and talk to neighbors and former owners if there are any. If possible, talk to people who were actually involved in the original incident which caused the ghostly legend to begin. As most origins are found in the distant past, this isn't always possible, however in tales of recent origin you may be able to locate an eyewitness or even someone directly involved. Find out all you can before going to the site, and talk to as many people who have experienced the ghost as you can. Try to ascertain if there is any motive for perpetrating a hoax. Most ghost stories, unfortunately, turn out to be hoaxes or mere urban legends. Many no longer occur, or, at least, haven't been seen in years. Try to find out how long its been since anyone experienced something at the site in question. If it's been very long, especially if people have been there in the intervening time, chances are you will not find anything going on.

Often, spooks do not show up with any regularity, being dormant for a while, then making a startling appearance. So, if you don't experience anything the first time at a site which is definitely still active, don't give up. It might take two or three times for the revenant to decide it's okay to come out.

Now that you have the essentials, good luck. Let me know if you find anything. You can contact me through my publisher. I would be happy to hear the results of any ghost hunt and to hear from anyone who has had an encounter of their own. I went on several amateur ghost hunts while in college. We found nothing more often than not, but we always had a good time. And we did find interesting things on a few occasions.

Be sure everyone is there for the right reasons. A party atmosphere is not conducive to what you are after in a ghost hunt. Make sure everyone understands to stay as quiet as possible and to closely observe any spectral activity. Someone crying out something like, "There's the ghost!" might shatter the mood and drive away the ghost. They can be flighty critters for things that go "bump in the night," and may simply vanish if startled or confronted in a hostile manner. Take care and good hunting.

Acknowledgments

First, I thank the Lord above for my talent to write and the patience to research and preserve these oral traditions. Second, I thank my parents, Flay and Katie Renegar who always supported all my endeavors with pride and love. I love you both. Thanks to my aunts, uncles, and cousins for patiently repeating the stories they remembered.

To Burt Calloway who planted the seed of an idea and encouraged me to undertake this writing, thanks for all your help. I couldn't have done it without your support.

Thank you to equestrian mystery writer Jody Jaffe for encouraging words. Thanks also to J. Michael Norman and Nancy Roberts for your time and encouragement.

To Cynthia Bright and Carol Bruckner of Bright Mountain Books: I appreciate your faith in the project. To Jean Reese who put much time and effort into this book, thank you so much for your ideas and all your hard work. God bless you!

Thanks to Shelia Burnsed and her daughter Kit. Thanks

also to David Crutchfield, Kelly Blackburn, Melanie and Brock Moore, Jenny Stoffle, Ron Gillespie, Kristen Crutchfield, Dennis Renfro, and all the "ghost chasers," my friends. And to Ronnie Filaromo and Alan McIntyre, two of my East Hall roommates, and Miriam and Michele Ribeiro and all the East Hall vets out there! To James Myers and Jennifer Norman for your hard work typing the original manuscript.

Thanks to Brandy Shutters and Stephanie Luffman for your time and efforts along the sides of "haunted" country lanes.

To my Great-aunt Nat, who went home to her Creator in June 2004; to Papa and Mammy (Lineberry), both two decades gone; and Grandpa George and Grandma Ruby Caroline Renegar, who I never knew; and finally, to Great-grandpas Shober and Charles: the yarns you spun will live forever!

To great memories,
Michael Renegar

Selected Bibliography

Calloway, Burt, and Jennifer FitzSimmons. *Triad Hauntings.* Winston-Salem, N.C.: Bandit Books, 1990.

Norman, Michael, and Beth Scott. *Haunted Heritage.* New York: Forge Books, Tom Doherty Associates LLC, 2002.

Roberts, Nancy. *Haunted Houses: Chilling Tales from 24 American Homes.* Guilford, Conn.: The Globe Pequot Press, 1998.

Roberts, Nancy. *North Carolina Ghosts & Legends.* Columbia, S.C.: University of South Carolina Press, 1991.

Russell, Randy, and Janet Barnett. *Mountain Ghost Stories and Curious Tales of Western North Carolina.* Winston-Salem, N.C.: John F. Blair, Publisher, 1988.

West, John Foster. *The Ballad of Tom Dula.* Boone, N.C.: Parkway Publishers, Inc., 2002.

Zepke, Terrance. *The Best Ghost Tales of North Carolina.* Sarasota, Fl.: Pineapple Press, Inc., 2001.

Michael F. Renegar

About the Author

Michael Renegar was raised in the small town of East Bend, North Carolina, where he still resides. He graduated from Forbush High School in 1987, and receiving a Sara Lee Scholarship, attended Appalachian State University in Boone, North Carolina.

While at Appalachian, Michael lived mostly in East Residence Hall, an old campus building reputed to be haunted. An earlier interest in ghosts and legends was renewed, and he began researching local "haunts" with friends and writing articles about their experiences.

Michael has always had a keen interest in the stories of his family and elders. Some of his fondest memories are of sitting and listening to his parents, grandparents, and various relatives tell tales of the past, including some harrowing ghost stories. Realizing that many of these stories might be lost, Michael set out to record as many as he could for future generations. In the process, he came across other stories and legends from the area, both historical and contemporary.

Other interests include photography, Tsarist Russia, history, coin collecting, playing guitar, songwriting, and Fifties Rock-n-Roll. Sherry Holly, niece of rock pioneer Buddy Holly, included one of Michael's songs on a gospel album released on her family's Cloud Nine record label.

Michael is always willing to share stores from his collection of spooky tales and stories of the old days. He is also always looking for new material to add to his ever-growing files, especially never-before-published accounts.